THE NORTH YORK MOORS

by

Paddy Dillon

CICERONE

2 POLICE SQUARE, MILNTHORPE, CUMBRIA LA7 7PY
www.cicerone.co.uk

Advice to Readers

Readers are advised that while every effort is taken by the author to
ensure the accuracy of this guidebook, changes can occur which may
affect the contents. It is advisable to check locally on transport, accommodation, shops, etc, but even rights of way can be altered. Paths can
be affected by forestry work, landslip or changes of ownership.

The author would welcome information on any updates and
changes sent through the publishers.

Front cover: The attrac

CONTENTS

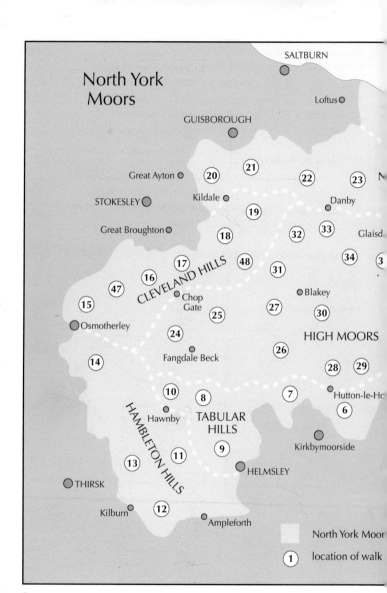

North York Moors

SALTBURN

Loftus

GUISBOROUGH

Great Ayton　(20)　(21)

STOKESLEY

Kildale

(19)

(22)　(23)　N

Danby

Great Broughton

(18)

(32)　(33)　Glaisd.

(17)　(48)

(16)

CLEVELAND HILLS

(31)　(34)　(3)

(47)

(15)

Chop Gate

(25)

Blakey

(27)

(30)

HIGH MOORS

(24)

Osmotherley

(14)

Fangdale Beck

(26)

(10)　(8)

(7)

(28)　(29)

Hutton-le-Ho

(6)

Hawnby

TABULAR HILLS

HAMBLETON HILLS

(11)

(9)

Kirkbymoorside

(13)

THIRSK

HELMSLEY

Kilburn　(12)

Ampleforth

North York Moor

(1)　location of walk

8

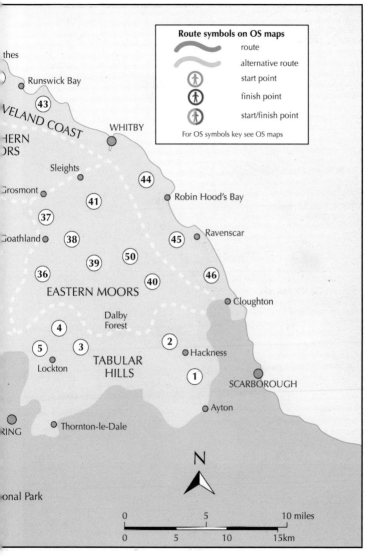

thes

Runswick Bay

(43)

VELAND COAST

WHITBY

HERN
ORS

Sleights

(44)

Grosmont

(41)

Robin Hood's Bay

(37)

Goathland

(38)

Ravenscar

(45)

(50)

(39)

(36)

(40)

(46)

EASTERN MOORS

Cloughton

Dalby
Forest

(4)

(2)

(5)

(3)

Hackness

Lockton

TABULAR
HILLS

(1)

SCARBOROUGH

Thornton-le-Dale

Ayton

RING

onal Park

N

Route symbols on OS maps

route

alternative route

start point

finish point

start/finish point

For OS symbols key see OS maps

0		5		10 miles
0	5		10	15km

Sheep grazing has ensured that the dales have been close cropped for centuries

INTRODUCTION

This guidebook offers 50 walks in the varied landscape of the North York Moors National Park. The park was designated in 1952 and covers 1432 square km (553 square miles) of land that comprise the largest continuous expanse of heather moorland in England. The moors are of no great height, yet offer a wonderful sense of spaciousness, with extensive views under a 'big sky'. There are also deep verdant dales where charming scenes and hoary stone buildings can be found, as well as a remarkable cliff coastline designated as heritage coast. The long-distance Cleveland Way wraps itself around the moors and coast, but there are many other walks that explore the rich variety of the area, focusing on its charm, history, heritage and wildlife.

The walks are distributed through seven regions within the park, enabling walkers to discover and appreciate the Tabular Hills, Hambleton Hills, Cleveland Hills, Northern Moors, High Moors, Eastern Moors and Cleveland coast. For those who like a challenge, the course of the classic Lyke Wake Walk, crossing the national park from east to west, is also offered, split over a four-day period to allow a leisurely appreciation of the moors. Almost 750km (465 miles) of walking routes are described here, though the national park could furnish many more splendid ones from a stock of 1770km (1100 miles) of public footpaths and bridleways.

People have crossed the North York Moors since time immemorial, and some of their routes survive to this day. Stout stone crosses were planted to assist travellers and traders with a safe passage, and these days practically all rights of way are signposted and walkable, though some routes are used far more than others.

Despite having the appearance of a wilderness, this has often been, and remains to this day, a working landscape. The moors are scarred and quarried in places by man's search for mineral resources, and the heather cover requires year-round management for the sport of grouse shooting. Walkers with enquiring minds will quickly realise that the human history and settlement of the moors, even at its highest points, stretches back over thousands of years. Our own enjoyment of the moors, in contrast, may be nothing more than a transient pleasure that leaves little trace.

Scenic dales are crisscrossed with field paths and farm tracks avoiding the roads

GETTING TO THE NORTH YORK MOORS

By Air and Sea

The nearest practical airports to the North York Moors are Leeds/Bradford and Teeside, though good rail connections allow ready access from the London airports and Manchester Airport. The nearest practical ferry ports are Hull and Newcastle.

By Rail

Good rail connections from around the country arrive at the busy tourist resort of Scarborough throughout the day. To a lesser extent, Whitby can be reached by direct rail services from Middlesbrough, which would suit most travellers from the Northeast. Other railway stations to consider include Malton, on account of its Moorsbus connections, and Saltburn, connecting with regular Arriva bus services. Check the rail website to plan journeys to and from the area – www.nationalrail.co.uk – or telephone National Rail Enquiries 08457 484950

By Bus

Daily National Express buses run to Scarborough and Whitby – www.nationalexpress.co.uk. Daily Yorkshire Coastliner buses run from Leeds and Bradford, through York, to Scarborough and Whitby – www.yorkshirecoastliner.co.uk. Daily Arriva bus services from the Northeast run to Guisborough, Whitby and Scarborough – www.arriva.co.uk. Daily East Yorkshire Motor Services buses run from Hull and the surrounding area to Scarborough – www.eyms.co.uk.

GETTING AROUND THE NORTH YORK MOORS

Some people, and this includes many walkers, seem loath to consider using public transport, but the sheer number of cars on the narrow roads in the North York Moors, filling car parks to capacity each summer, is a problem that needs to be addressed. There are good transport services in the area, and with a bit of careful thought and planning there is no need for a car. Indeed, the author researched this guidebook using only public transport, and seemed to cover a lot more ground than many people who based their explorations around the 'convenience' of their car!

Moorsbus

The Moorsbus is a network of special low-cost bus services, often tying in with other bus services to link some of the more popular little towns and villages with some of the more remote parts of the national park. Walkers who wish to make use of Moorsbus services should obtain a current timetable either from the national park authority or from tourist information centres. Timetables and places served do tend to change each year, so it is essential to obtain up-to-date information. Copies of timetables also contain plenty of other useful information for travellers, as well as vouchers for discounts at visitor attractions, accommodation, shops, restaurants and galleries. Moorsbus services can also be checked on the website – **www.moors.uk.net/moorsbus**.

Buses

Other bus services are also available in the national park. Arriva buses run

Moorsbus offers regular services linking towns and villages with dales and moors

The North Yorkshire Moors Railway provides nostalgic steam-hauled services

excellent regular daily services around the northern part of the North York Moors, as well as along the coast from Staithes to Whitby and Scarborough. Scarborough & District buses cover the southern parts of the North York Moors, between Scarborough and Helmsley, and along the coast from Scarborough to Ravenscar. Details can be checked on the websites – www.arriva.co.uk and www.eyms.co.uk. Finally, there are several small operators who may run no more than occasional minibus services linking a few villages to one of the market towns.

Rail

Following the closure of the coastal line in 1965, rail services have been drastically cut back in the North York Moors. However, Arriva trains run along the Eskdale line from Middlesbrough to Whitby, providing access to a series of fine walks in the northern part of the national park. Seasonal steam-hauled services on the North York Moors Railway between Pickering and Goathland catch the attention of walkers who want to enjoy nostalgic railway access to their walks. And all was not completely lost with the closure of the coastal railway, since the entire line between Scarborough and Whitby is now available as a walking and cycling route! Arriva train times can be checked at www.arriva.co.uk, while North Yorkshire Moors Railway services can be found at www.northyorkshiremoorsrailway.com.

Traveline and Taxis

To check any type of public transport throughout the North York Moors, simply call Traveline on 0870 6082608. There is also a leaflet called Moors Explorer which shows all services at a glance. It is published annually and available from tourist information centres. Walkers who wish to contact a taxi could try phoning the National Taxi Hotline free on 0800 654321. This will put you in touch with the nearest taxi operator in the scheme and you can negotiate your trip and check the price straight away.

ACCOMMODATION

Accommodation options around the North York Moors National Park are abundant, but bear in mind that during the peak summer season it can still be difficult to secure lodgings, and in the depths of winter some places are not open. At the budget end there are plenty of campsites, although youth hostels are rather thin on the ground. Following closures in recent years there is now only Whitby, Boggle Hole, Scarborough, Lockton, Helmsley and Osmotherley. In addition, an independent hostel is available at Whitby, and a handful of basic camping barns are dotted around the national park.

Walkers looking for bed and breakfast, guest house or hotel accommodation will find plenty of choice in some areas, especially the coastal resorts, but little or nothing in some of the less-frequented dales further inland. However, every standard is available, from homely bed and breakfasts and basic farmhouse accommodation, to luxury hotels with every facility and full meals services. On the whole, serviced accommodation in the North York Moors tends to be a little pricey, but with careful searching reasonably priced options can be found. During the peak summer season and at busy weekends you can save a lot of time by directing your enquiry through a tourist information centre. Some of these centres will book accommodation for you, either when you turn up in person, or over the telephone if you can quote a credit card number.

FOOD AND DRINK

Most of the walking routes in this guidebook start and finish at places where food and drink are available. The starting point may be a town with plenty of pubs, restaurants and cafés, or it may be a village with only one or two pubs and a tea room. There may be places en route that offer food and drink, such as wayside pubs and cafés, or occasionally there may be nothing at all, though a nearby town or village might be visited after completing the walk. A note about the availability of refreshments is given in the information box at the beginning of each walk, though there is no guarantee that the places will be open at

15

the point where you actually need them! When booking accommodation be sure to enquire at an early stage if you require meals, or to let your hosts know that you are on a special diet, rather than leaving it too late and having to go hungry. It goes without saying that you should be self-sufficient for food and drink for the duration of your walks.

WHEN TO WALK

Most visitors – and indeed *too many* visitors – explore the North York Moors in the summer months, and when the moors are flushed purple with heather and the air is sweetened with its scent, this can be a delightful time. But be warned that when the sun beats down on the moors there may be little shade, and the longer a heatwave lasts, the more the air tends to turn hazy, so that colour and depth is lost from the views. The spring and autumn months offer better walking conditions, with plenty of cool, clear days – often cool enough to ensure that you keep striding briskly! There is also less pressure on accommodation and easier access to attractions along the way. In the winter months backup facilities such as accommodation and transport are much reduced, and foul weather can sweep across the moors, which offer little shelter from wind or rain.

The High Moors seem to stretch forever and may lack prominent landmark features

16

However, there can be some exceptionally bright and clear days, and a dusting of snow on the landscape transforms the scene into something quite magical. (When there is too much snow it tends to accumulate in deep drifts that can be difficult to negotiate, but such conditions are rare.)

MAPS OF THE ROUTES

Extracts from the Ordnance Survey Landranger series of maps, at a scale of 1:50 000, are used throughout this guidebook, with overlays showing the routes. These extracts are adequate for navigation on the walks, but if you wish to explore more of the countryside off-route, and see exactly where you are in relation to other walking routes, then you will need the appropriate Ordnance Survey maps. The Landranger maps covering the North York Moors National Park include sheets 93, 94, 99, 100 and 101. Greater detail and clarity is available using Ordnance Survey Explorer maps, at a scale of 1:25 000. The relevant Explorer maps are OL26, covering the western half of the national park, and OL27, covering the eastern half of the national park. Bear in mind that these maps are printed on both sides, so that each sheet has a North and South side. The relevant Ordnance Survey maps for each walk are quoted in the information box introducing the walk. The starting points for the walks can be pinpointed using the six-figure Ordnance Survey grid references supplied.

Use up-to-date maps, as dozens of rights of way have been officially diverted over the years, often to avoid either farmyards or cutting across fields of crops. On the high moors walkers who are good map-readers will frequently notice that the clear path or track they are following is not actually a right of way, and that the route shown on the map as a right of way is in fact quite untrodden on the ground! What to do? It seems that most walkers are happy to vote with their feet and follow the clear paths and tracks, and most landowners seem happy for them to continue doing so. The most up-to-date maps will show vast areas that are available under the so-called 'freedom to roam' arrangement. While the 'freedom' may be there most of the time, it can be curtailed when land management and other activities require it. Not all walkers would relish trekking through deep heather! For current access conditions check the relevant website – **www.countrysideaccess.gov.uk**.

NATIONAL PARK VISITOR CENTRES

There are two national park visitor centres in the North York Moors, and they perform the very important function of trying to interest visitors in and educate them about the necessary balance that needs to be struck between conservation and recreation in this fragile upland area. The busier of the two centres

Ralph Cross is an ancient moorland marker and serves as the national park logo

*When the mist rolls across the moors
do you have the necessary skills to continue?*

is beside the main road at the top of Sutton Bank, the quieter one is outside the little village of Danby in Eskdale. Both centres are full of information, dispensing maps, guidebooks and leaflets covering walking opportunities, as well as presenting the history, heritage and natural history of the area. There are audio-visual presentations, as well as guided walks with national park rangers. One of the pressing concerns in the North York Moors National Park is to try to reduce the number of vehicles that clog the narrow roads and overflow from every car park during the summer season. To this end, both centres are regularly visited by Moorsbus services, and the message is continually plugged that people should be using public transport.

National Park Centre, Sutton Bank, ☎ 01845 597426.
The Moors Centre, Danby, ☎ 01287 660654.

For administrative enquiries contact: North York Moors National Park Authority, The Old Vicarage, Bondgate, Helmsley, York, YO62 5BP.
Website for the North York Moors National Park – **www.moors.uk.net**.

19

TOURIST INFORMATION CENTRES

Tourist information centres in and around the North York Moors National Park are keen to help visitors with all sorts of enquiries, such as accommodation, attractions, transport, etc. Many of them have plenty of information to give away, or sell, and some will handle bookings on your behalf. Tourist information centres along the walking routes are mentioned throughout the guidebook, but the following is a complete list:

Great Ayton, High Green Car Park,
☎ 01642 722835
Guisborough, Priory Grounds,
☎ 01287 633801
Helmsley, Market Place,
☎ 01439 770173
Hutton-le-Hole, Ryedale Folk Museum,
☎ 01751 417367
Low Dalby, Forest Visitor Centre,
☎ 01751 460295
Pickering, The Ropery,
☎ 01751 473791
Scarborough, Valley Bridge Road,
☎ 01723 373333
Thirsk, Market Place,
☎ 01845 522755
Whitby, Langbourne Road,
☎ 01947 602674

EMERGENCY SERVICES

No matter what the nature of the emergency, if it requires the police, ambulance, fire service, mountain rescue or coastguard, the number to dial is 999. (The European number 112 also connects to the emergency services.) Be ready to give a full account of the nature of the emergency, and give your own phone number so that they can stay in contact with you. Callers cannot request things like helicopter assistance, and whether the use of one is appropriate will be determined by the information supplied about the emergency. All walkers should carry a basic first-aid kit to deal with minor incidents, be self-sufficient in terms of food and drink, and dress in or carry appropriate clothing to cover for whatever the weather is likely to be. When venturing into remote country or encountering difficult situations, walkers either need the experience and skills to deal with the situation, or the common sense to turn back at an early stage. Think about your actions and aim to walk safely.

THE TABULAR HILLS

The Tabular Hills stretch along the southern part of the North York Moors National Park. The land rises gently from south to north, and is cut by a series of dales that leave 'tabular' uplands between them. The gentle slope often ends abruptly at its northern end in a series of shapely knolls, or 'nabs', that look out towards the rolling moorlands at the heart of the national park. From east to west, from Scarborough to Helmsley, the more prominent 'nabs' include: Barns Cliff, Langdale Rigg End, Blakey Topping, Whinny Nab, Levisham Moor, the Nab, Boonhill Common, Birk Nab, Helmsley Bank, Easterside Hill and Hawnby Hill. Prominent dales from east to west include: the Forge Valley, Hole of Horcum, Newtondale, lower Rosedale, lower Farndale, Sleightholm Dale, Riccal Dale, Ash Dale, Beck Dale and lower Ryedale.

The rocks making up the Tabular Hills are seldom exposed, but belong to the middle oolite group in the Corallian series of the Jurassic period and hence are around 170 million years old. They are essentially a limestone and lime-rich-sandstone series, porous enough to allow surface water to drain away rapidly. In the more deeply cut dales the bedrock is the older Oxford clay, which is impervious and supports the flow of rivers and streams. While some parts of the Tabular Hills have been turned over to commercial forestry, the land is very fertile and easily ploughed, although the soil is often too thin to support good root crops. But grain crops such as wheat, barley and oats are grown in rotation, and oilseed rape blazes yellow early in summer.

As if to celebrate the distinct nature of these gentle heights, the waymarked Tabular Hills Walk has been established. It traverses the low hills and intervening dales from the coast at Scalby Mills to the bustling market town of Helmsley, a distance of 80km (50 miles). The signposts and waymarks for the route feature directional arrows and a 'Tabular Hills' logo. The route has been designated a regional trail and is an initiative of the North York Moors National Park Authority.

Ten walking routes through the Tabular Hills are described, including: two around Hackness, three in the Lockton and Levisham area, and one each around Hutton-le-Hole, Gillamoor, Rievaulx Moor, Helmsley and Hawnby. Some of these take in the distinctive 'nabs' while others wander more through the dales. From time to time, on the higher ground, it is possible to look along the range and see how the higher 'nabs' end abruptly and the High Moors then stretch northwards into the heart of the North York Moors.

WALK 1

West Ayton, Hackness and the Forge Valley

Distance	15km (9.5 miles)
Start/finish	Forge Valley Inn, West Ayton, GR 987847
Maps	OS Landranger 101; OS Explorer OL27 South
Terrain	Easy walking along woodland paths and field paths, along with farm tracks and minor roads
Refreshments	Ye Olde Forge Valley Inn at West Ayton, East Ayton Country Hotel and Denison Arms at East Ayton, Everley Country Hotel is off-route between Mowthorpe and Hackness, and Hackness. Grange Hotel is off-route near Hackness.
Transport	Regular Scarborough & District buses serve West Ayton from Scarborough, Pickering and Helmsley, and there are occasional Moorsbus services to Hackness and the Forge Valley from Thornton-le-Dale and West Ayton

The River Derwent once flowed straight from the moors to the sea, but at the end of the ice age its course was blocked and water overflowed to cut the Forge Valley, which was later choked by wildwoods. These trees were harvested for charcoal to fuel small ironworks in the 14th century. The River Derwent repeatedly flooded the low-lying Vale of Pickering, so in the 18th century the Sea Cut was engineered to take the river along its original course to the sea. This walk explores the wooded Forge Valley, takes a look at the Sea Cut and offers the chance to visit the lovely estate village of Hackness.

Start at Ye Olde Forge Valley Inn at **West Ayton**. Follow the main A170 across the bridge to **East Ayton** and turn left along a road called **Castlegate**, signposted for the Forge Valley. Pass the **East Ayton Country Hotel** and walk down the road. Follow the road until a **public footpath** is signposted on the right, flanked by fencing for a few paces. Continue uphill along a woodland track and avoid a turning to the left to climb up through a deep groove instead. Turn left near the top of the wooded slope and follow a path that stays just inside the woodland, parallel to the edge, with occasional views out across fields. Pass attractive pantiled stone buildings at **Osborne Lodge** and walk straight ahead. Fork left down to a viewpoint, where an information board explains how the Forge Valley was formed.

FORGE VALLEY WOODS NATIONAL NATURE RESERVE

Towards the end of the ice age, around 10,000 years ago, a mass of stagnant ice dammed the broad valley, causing water to form the temporary Lake Hackness. This overflowed and carved the deep, steep-sided Forge Valley. The fields above the valley lie on soft Hambleton oolite, while its sides are hard lower calcareous grit, and its floor is impervious Oxford clay. The valley became choked with wildwoods, which in turn provided charcoal for small iron foundries in the 14th century. This is one of the best valley-side mixed deciduous woodlands in Yorkshire.

The Sea Cut uses the original course of the River Derwent from Mowthorpe Bridge

Continue down the path, passing a **small quarry**. The path steepens then levels out. Another information board explains how non-native beech, larch and sycamore are being felled to encourage more varied ground cover and habitats. The path swings down to the right to reach a parking space at **Green Gate**. Turn left, then right down a road sign-posted for Hackness, where there is access to the **Hazel Head Picnic Site**, which offers views of the valley. Walk down the road to cross **Mowthorpe Bridge** over the Sea Cut.

THE SEA CUT

The River Derwent has its source on Fylingdales Moor, a mere spit and a throw from the North Sea. It begins by flowing towards the sea, but only 6km (4 miles) short of it, suddenly swings west and heads far inland. Its waters eventually spill into the North Sea via the Humber Estuary after a circuitous journey of 240km (150 miles). The Sea Cut, engineered by the distinguished inventor Sir George Cayley (a pioneer in the science of aerodynamics, amongst other things) in the early 18th century, diverts the headwaters of the River Derwent into Scalby Beck, passing floodwater straight to the sea instead of allowing it to inundate the Vale of Pickering.

Pass **Mowthorpe Farm** and walk a little way up the road, then turn right as indicated by a footpath sign. Go through a kissing gate and turn right to walk downhill a little, then turn left to walk up a grassy groove alongside an old hedgerow. Go through a gate, then turn left up to another gate that gives access to **Hawthorn Wood**. Follow a clear path across and up the wooded slope then walk beside a field to reach **Suffield Ings farm** around 160m (525ft). Keep to the right of the buildings as marked and leave along the farm access road. Keep straight on at a junction, but later, when the track swings right, leave it by following a path down to the left. This goes down a wooded valley and passes a crumbling **limekiln**. When a road is reached, turn left, and you don't even have to walk on the road, since as one path joins it, another heads off to the left. Note that the village of **Hackness** is easily reached from here, allowing a link with Walk 2.

The path climbs a wooded slope then runs up a grassy slope, apparently for no other reason than to enjoy a fine view of **Hackness Hall**. Having achieved this aim the path turns right downhill, crosses a stile and enters a wood, then cuts gradually downhill across a slope. Leave the wood at another stile and contour across a grassy slope overlooking **Mill Farm** and the Derwent Valley. Turn right downhill as marked to cross a road and then a nearby footbridge over the River Derwent. Walk straight ahead alongside a field to reach the hamlet of **Wrench Green**. Follow an access road past some cottages, then turn left along a minor road. Keep straight ahead at a junction marked 'No through road'. Pass more cottages at **Cockrah House**.

Walk a little way uphill and keep left to cross a cattle-grid where a track is marked for **North Stile Cottage**. Don't walk along the track, but drift slightly left across a pathless grassy slope, as if heading directly through the valley. Stiles and markers appear only when fences and hedges need crossing, and the route runs roughly parallel to the **River Derwent**. Pass the point where the **Sea Cut** takes water from the river, leaving only a diminutive Derwent.

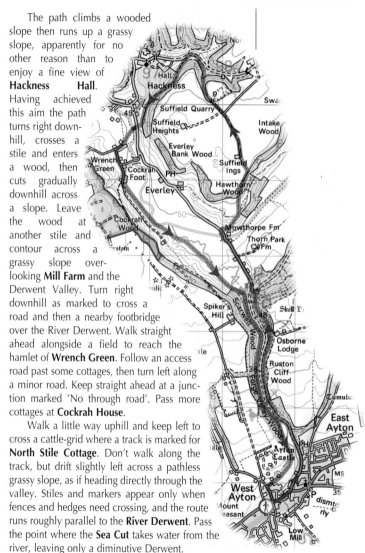

The duck-board riverside path through the jungle-like woods in the Forge Valley

Walk beside the River Derwent, but avoid muddy patches and gorse by drifting uphill a little. Enter the **Forge Valley Woods** again, following a clear duckboard path parallel to the river. There is access to a car park across a **footbridge**, where an information board illustrates local wildlife. If the car park is not required there is no need to cross the river, and the duckboard path can be followed further downstream. The woodlands are dense and the undergrowth lush, so the route is rather like a jungle trek!

The duckboard ends suddenly at a **gate and stile**. Walk through a narrow meadow between the river and a wooded slope. Near the end of the meadow watch out for a track heading up to the right. Go through a gate and follow the grassy track past the tottering 14th-century ruins of **Ayton Castle**, then continue along a road past cottages at **Castle Rise**. Turn left down **Yedmandale Road** to return to the main road and Ye Olde Forge Valley Inn at **West Ayton**.

WALK 2
Hackness, Broxa and Whisper Dale

Distance	10km (6 miles)
Start/finish	Hackness village hall, GR 967900
Maps	OS Landrangers 94 and 101; OS Explorer OL27 South
Terrain	Tracks and paths on wooded slopes and through fields
Refreshments	Hackness Grange Hotel is near the start
Transport	Occasional Moorsbus services to Hackness from Thornton-le-Dale and West Ayton, connecting with regular Scarborough & District buses

Hackness is a charming little village with a long history – the Abbess Hilda of Whitby chose a secluded site here for a nunnery. A few quiet, charming and often unregarded little dales fan outwards from the village into surrounding forest, and a couple are explored on this short walk. The route starts with a climb onto broad, cultivated Broxa Rigg, with a descent to Hard Dale and High Dales. After crossing Springwood Heights, Whisper Dale is a sinuous grassy valley leading down to Low Dales on the return journey to Hackness.

Starting at **Hackness village hall**, walk up the road as if heading for the rest of the village, then double back sharp left up a track on a wooded slope. Keep right at a track junction to reach a grassy crest. Stay beside **Chapman Banks Wood** for a while, drifting right to avoid nettles and thistles, and go through a gap in a low stone wall. Keep to the woodland edge on the other side of the **Broxa Rigg** crest, around 160m (525ft), looking carefully in the corner of the field to spot a step-stile. Keep to the field edges, beside the wood, to cross other step-stiles. In the last field, aim for a farmhouse to cross another stile.

Keep right of the buildings at **Broxa** to follow a broad, clear farm road. Turn right along a narrow, tarmac, muck-and-manure road and follow this, passing a public

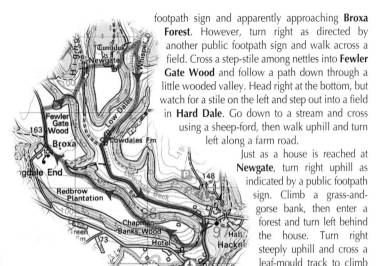

footpath sign and apparently approaching **Broxa Forest**. However, turn right as directed by another public footpath sign and walk across a field. Cross a step-stile among nettles into **Fewler Gate Wood** and follow a path down through a little wooded valley. Head right at the bottom, but watch for a stile on the left and step out into a field in **Hard Dale**. Go down to a stream and cross using a sheep-ford, then walk uphill and turn left along a farm road.

Just as a house is reached at **Newgate**, turn right uphill as indicated by a public footpath sign. Climb a grass-and-gorse bank, then enter a forest and turn left behind the house. Turn right steeply uphill and cross a leaf-mould track to climb further. Leave the forest and walk alongside a field, continuing beside another stand of forest around 160m (525ft). Veer right as signposted 'Whisperdales', near **Springwood Cottage**, to go down into another wood. Swing left down a clear woodland track and branch right at the bottom alongside a fence. Step out into a field and head diagonally down it to reach a grassy track in **Whisper Dale** beside a stream flanked by trees.

The grassy track running downhill from Whisper Dale towards Lowdales

Turn right to follow the grassy track down through the valley. It remains grassy and is marked by arrows for a while. Cross two footbridges beside two fords close together at **Lowdales**. Follow a field path to the left of the road, as the road actually carries the full flow of water from **Lowdales Beck**! Continue to follow the road down through the dale to reach a junction. Left leads to St Peter's Church in Hackness, while right takes you back to the road junction at the **village hall**, not far from the Hackness Grange Hotel.

Hackness Hall and Hackness village with a view along the length of Lowdales

HACKNESS

St Hilda founded a nunnery at Hackness in 680 AD, but even in this secluded setting it was discovered and plundered by the Danes in 867 AD, then rebuilt in the 11th century. An inscribed cross from the nunnery is located in St Peter's Church, but the only other reminder of those times is the village pond. Hackness is very much an estate village, and its main street is peculiar, as it has a vigorous stream running alongside it. Hackness Hall is a fine Georgian manor designed by John Carr, an architect from York. The hall is in the possession of Lord Derwent.

WALK 3
Lockton, Stain Dale, Saltergate and Levisham Moor

Distance	20km (12.5 miles)
Start/finish	Lockton Youth Hostel, GR 845900
Maps	OS Landranger 94; OS Explorer OL27 South
Terrain	Generally easy, but a long walk; woodland tracks and field paths in the lower dales give way to higher moorland paths and tracks
Refreshments	Saltergate Inn at Saltergate Bank, Horseshoe Inn at Levisham, the Pantry café at Lockton
Transport	Regular Yorkshire Coastliner buses serve Lockton and Saltergate from Pickering and Whitby

Lockton and Levisham lie within easy reach of deep dales and open moorlands. This fine, long walk leaves Lockton and drops down into Stain Dale, then later climbs to reach strangely sculpted rocks at the Bride Stones. Newgate Brow and Saltergate Brow allow wide-ranging views across the moors and dales, then there is an opportunity to take a break at the Legendary Saltersgate Inn. An easy walk over Levisham Moor leads to the charming stone village of Levisham, which surrounds a spacious green. The route closes by crossing a deep, wooded dale to return to Lockton.

Leave **Lockton** and its eco-friendly youth hostel by heading for the main **A169**, as if going directly to Saltergate. Cross the main road to enter a field. Don't follow the clear track, but strike diagonally right across the field. There is no path, but keep to the right of a **pylon** to find a track leading down through a gate. Go down the track into a wood and pass through a handful of gates. Watch carefully, as the route avoids **Staindale Lodge** in the following manner: turn right as marked up a grassy slope,

The top-heavy Pepperpot is one of many natural sculptures at the Bride Stones

turn right up an access road to a gate and cross a stile over a wall, turn left to follow a track through a wood, and on leaving the wood turn left down to **Staindale Lodge**. Turn left again and cross a couple of stiles, then go through gates to pass outbuildings.

Follow a grassy path through **Holm Woods**, noting the telegraph poles that run parallel.

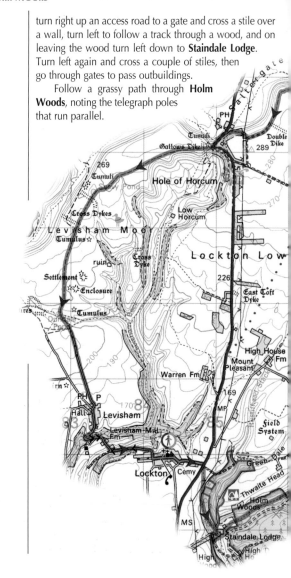

Continue walking through meadows, using the telegraph poles as guides when looking ahead to spot gates and stiles. Pass to the right of the buildings at **Low Staindale** and follow a grassy track down to ford a stream. Turn left to go through a kissing gate and enter little Dovedale, with its ancient oak woodland and flower-rich grasslands. Cross a little footbridge and walk along the grassy floor of the dale. Cross another little footbridge and follow a stone-paved path up a ridge called **Needle Point**. This is sparsely wooded, with a lush ground cover of heather and bilberry. The path levels out and runs through a groove in the heather, then a sandy path leads to the **High Bride Stones**, around 200m (655ft). Turn right here, away from the oddly sculpted rocks, to follow the path into a little valley full of birch and bushy bilberry. Climb uphill a little and swing right to pass the **Low Bride Stones**, including the deeply undercut, top-heavy **Pepperpot**.

Turn left along a clear path and keep left at junctions with other paths. A clear track runs onwards, with **Dalby Forest** to the right and scrub moorland to the left. Keep to this track, rising very gently as it proceeds, to reach an improved pasture on **Newgate Moor**. Turn slightly left to follow another track along the top of wooded **Newgate Brow**, with the hump of Blakey Topping prominently in view. Watch carefully to spot a narrow path slicing down to the right, later – an old **stone gatepost** partly buried in the undergrowth helps identify it. Follow this path down across the

33

THE NORTH YORK MOORS

The leaning stone pillar of Malo Cross and the rounded hump of Whinny Nab

wooded slope and continue along its foot, keeping left of farm buildings at **Newgate Foot**.

Cross stiles on either side of the access road and turn left along a grassy terrace. Watch carefully for a small gate on the right and walk down through a squelchy field to a large gate. Follow a path that gradually drifts away from a forest, going through more gates as a couple of big thistle fields give way to bracken moorland. Reach the prominent leaning stone pillar of **Malo Cross** at a junction of paths.

Turn left alongside a fence as signposted for Horcum. The path rises from a slope of scrub woodland and bracken to the top of a fine grassy brow. (Alternatively, climb straight from the stone cross onto **Whinny Nab**, at 296m (971ft), then continue along the brow.) Either way, keep walking along the grassy brow, with views down to the Saltersgate Inn. Go through a gate and later enter a shelter belt forest at another gate. Turn right to follow a path beneath a **pylon line**, then down a groove on a forested slope to land on the main A169 near the **Saltersgate Inn.**

Walk up busy **Saltergate Bank**, using the right-hand side of the road, facing oncoming traffic for safety. Reach a gap at the head of the **Hole of Horcum** to look down into the deep dalehead. Turn right to follow a moorland track a short way uphill – it soon levels out around 270m

THE LEGENDARY SALTERSGATE INN

Saltergate was an important trading route running inland from the coast. It was also known as the 'Salt Road' or 'Fish Road'. Smugglers took illicit goods along it and were in the habit of holing up at the Saltersgate Inn. According to local lore, revenue men raided the place one night, but the smugglers ensured that nothing was discovered. However, one revenue man who lingered too long afterwards was killed and his body buried beneath the hearthstone of the inn. The landlord of the day insisted that a fire be kept continually ablaze to deter anyone from digging up the hearthstone, and this tradition was maintained for generations afterwards. The ever-blazing fire at the inn became a tourist attraction in its own right!

(885ft) on **Levisham Moor**. There is only one clear track across the undulating heather moorland, so route-finding errors are unlikely, even though the area is quite featureless. Small cast-iron plaques mark features of interest along the way, e.g. tiny **Seavy Pond** and **Dundale Pond**, dug in medieval times as watering-holes for livestock, and which might easily be passed unseen, choked as they are with vegetation.

The track crosses a gap at the latter, then forges a short way uphill to leave the moorland at a gate, where it becomes a tarmac road, **Limpsey Gate Lane**, leading down into the attractive and spacious village of **Levisham**. Keep walking down the road, out of the village. The road drops in a steep zigzag to pass **Levisham Mill**, deep in the valley, then climbs up the steep road on the other side to return to **Lockton**.

LEVISHAM AND LOCKTON

Levisham boasts a broad central green surrounded by stout stone cottages and farmhouses. Facilities include the Horseshoe Inn for food, drink and accommodation, as well as farmhouse and country house accommodation and a post office. An eco-friendly youth hostel is available at Lockton, which also has the Pantry shop and café. The road between the two villages features 1:5 gradients on both sides of the valley.

WALK 4
Levisham and the Hole of Horcum

Distance	13km (8 miles)
Start/finish	Horseshoe Inn, Levisham, GR 833906
Maps	OS Landranger 94 or 100; OS Explorer OL27 South
Terrain	Valley-side paths cross steep wooded slopes as well as gentler moorland ones, with easier field paths towards the end; generally easy
Refreshments	Horseshoe Inn at Levisham, Saltersgate Inn is just off-route on Saltergate Bank
Transport	None to Levisham; regular Yorkshire Coastliner buses serve Lockton and Saltergate from Pickering and Whitby, and Levisham Railway Station offers an alternative starting point for those using the North Yorkshire Moors Railway

The village of Levisham is reached only after negotiating 1:5 gradient roads – anyone going there by car has to leave the same way. Deep, steep-sided valleys flank Levisham Moor, while the Hole of Horcum is a remarkable dalehead that was carved by glacial melt-water at the end of the ice age. Most visitors come and go using the main road over Saltergate Bank, but the Hole of Horcum can be reached by using valley-side paths from Levisham. The return to Levisham via Levisham Bottoms overlooks part of the North Yorkshire Moors Railway.

Leave the Horseshoe Inn at the top end of **Levisham** and walk straight down through the village, admiring the stone houses that surround the broad central green. Pass the **Moorlands Country House** to leave the village. Turn left down a footpath that swings left across a wooded slope. Later, climb steps, then fork left at a junction along a path signposted for Horcum. The path is quite narrow and flanked by flowers, brambles and bracken, with views across the valley to the village of **Lockton**.

The path swings left as it works its way through the valley, and is well wooded at times along **Levisham Brow**. Generally, the path runs gradually downhill and the woods begin to thin out. Go through a small gate and cut across a slope of bracken to reach the side-valley of **Dundas Griff**. A signpost points ahead to Saltergate and a small stream has to be forded, then you cross **Levisham Beck** using a footbridge.

Follow the path gently uphill, across the wooded valley side, crossing a couple of stiles. Continue along a sheep path across the grassy valley side, and later keep to the left of the building at **Low Horcum**. Walk onwards and head down a grassy track to go through a gate. A clear path leads up through heather, then rises more steeply up a heathery groove as it climbs out of the

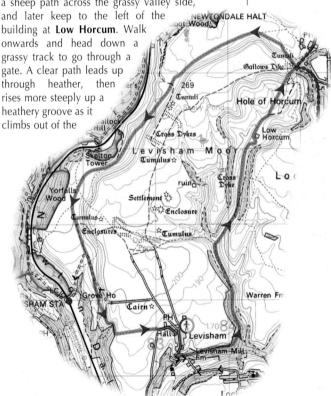

A clear path climbs up through the heathery head of the Hole of Horcum

Hole of Horcum. Enjoy the views around this splendid hollow, then cross a ladder stile at the top to see a bend in the busy main road on **Saltergate Bank**.

HOLE OF HORCUM

According to a locally favoured legend, a giant by the name of Wade who was out of sorts with his wife scooped up a pile of earth to throw at her, and missed. The resulting hole became the Hole of Horcum, while the lump of earth became Blakey Topping. From a gap at the head of the Hole of Horcum the Legendary Saltersgate Inn can be seen, and is easily visited if food and drink are required. The strange pyramidal radar at RAF Fylingdales rises beyond, looking quite out of place in the bleak moorland setting.

A gate and stile give access to a track rising from the road. (See Walk 3 for a quick return to Levisham.) Cross the stile, but turn immediately right to cross another stile and slant left downhill. Walk across a grassy moor, but don't stray too far from the steep slopes of **Levisham Moor**. There is a vague path, which becomes much clearer later, but take the time to spot it instead of forging straight through the heather. Later there is more bracken, then views down on the North Yorkshire Moors Railway in the deep gorge of Newtondale. A short detour could be made to the little ruin of **Skelton Tower**, which is a good viewpoint overlooking the gorge, but return to the main path afterwards. The path is broad and grassy and eventually reaches a bend on a minor road above **Levisham Railway Station**. (The station offers an alternative starting point.)

Walk up the road, but only to pass a small wood. Branch off to the right, but fork left almost immediately to follow a grassy path. Further along turn left up another clear grassy path, climbing up a slope covered in gorse bushes. Turn easily around the top of a small, steep-sided wooded valley, then walk alongside a couple of large fields. Follow a narrow road straight into **Levisham** to return to the Horseshoe Inn.

Skelton Tower overlooks Newtondale
and the North Yorkshire Moors Railway

WALK 5
Levisham Station, Levisham
and Newton-on-Rawcliffe

Distance	10km (6 miles)
Start/finish	Levisham Railway Station, GR 818910
Maps	OS Landranger 94 or 100; OS Explorer OL27 South
Terrain	Generally easy, using clear roads and tracks for most of the way, with a steep, vague and possibly muddy path at the end
Refreshments	Horseshoe Inn at Levisham, tea garden at Farwath, Mucky Duck at Newton-on-Rawcliffe
Transport	The seasonal North Yorkshire Moors Railway serves Levisham Railway Station; occasional Moorsbus and Hutchinsons buses serve Newton-on-Rawcliffe from Pickering

Levisham Railway Station is on the North Yorkshire Moors Railway – a nostalgic seasonal steam line through the heathery heart of the North York Moors National Park. The station lies deep in the dale, well below the village of Levisham, and even less conveniently situated at the foot of a steep slope from the village of Newton-on-Rawcliffe. This short circular walk climbs from Levisham Station to Levisham, then runs down a wooded valley to Farwath. After climbing to Newton-on-Rawcliffe, the route drops steeply to the station.

Leave **Levisham Railway Station** by following the road as if for Levisham village, but only to pass **Grove Lodge**. Just as the road begins to steepen, head off to the right through a small gate and follow a path up a wooded slope. Walk up a field to go through a gate at the top, then turn right. Almost immediately, fork left up a grassy path on a slope of gorse bushes. Turn easily around the top of a small, steep-sided wooded valley, then walk alongside a couple of big fields around 190m (625ft). Follow a narrow road into **Levisham** to reach the Horseshoe Inn at the top end of the village.

Walk down the road through a spacious green surrounded by stone farms and cottages. Pass the **Moorlands Country House** at the bottom end of the village, then walk down the steep zigzag road into a wooded valley. Turn right along a track signposted as the Tabular Hills Walk, and walk to a ruined church.

LEVISHAM CHURCH

St Mary's Church, on an 11th-century foundation, seems rather remote from Levisham village, tucked deep in a steep-sided valley. According to legend it was supposed to be built in the village, but each night the devil carried all the building materials down into the valley! The church was virtually abandoned before the tower was added, and a new church was built in 1884 at a more convenient location in the village.

Cross a small footbridge beyond the church, then turn right up a narrow path on a wooded slope. Turn right again along a track, passing through sloping fields using gates. One stretch runs through a wood, then on leaving the wood swing right to reach **Farwath**. A marshy grassland nearby is the Hagg Wood Marsh Nature Reserve, where alkaline waters allow an interesting assemblage of plants to flourish. Either take a break at the **Farwath Tea Gardens**, or cross both the railway line and **Pickering Beck** to leave.

Walk up a track on a steep wooded slope. Note a footpath signpost pointing right, but keep walking up the track to reach a junction at the top, above the woods. Turn right along a farm road

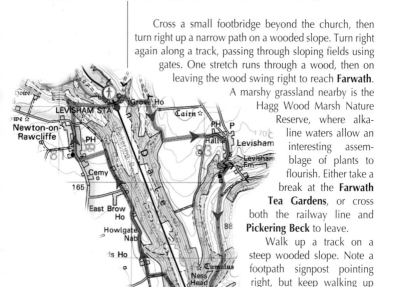

and follow this straight ahead, passing **Howlgate Farm** and **East Brow House**, until eventually a public footpath sign points left. Turn left and walk through a field and along a path leading to St John's Church. Turn right to follow a road through **Newton-on-Rawcliffe**. There are a lodgings here, while the Mucky Duck pub faces a duck pond.

The Mucky Duck pub and the little village duck pond at Newton-on-Rawcliffe

Follow the road to the top of the village and keep to a grassy track just to the right of a stone seat, as signposted for Cropton. Cross a rise at 190m (625ft) and drop down past a building, descending a steep hollow-way on a wooded slope. Watch for a stile on the right and cross it to head off to the right, descending very gradually across the slope into **Newtondale**, looking out for a gate. Go through the gate and veer left, looking into the valley to spot **Levisham Railway Station**, then find a path leading off the grassy slope and steeply down a wooded slope – this can be muddy when wet. Cross a footbridge to return to the station.

NORTH YORK MOORS RAILWAY

This scenic railway runs between Pickering and Grosmont, a distance of 29km (18 miles), and is famous for its steam-hauled services, though when it first opened in 1836 the carriages were actually horse-drawn between Pickering and Whitby. George Stephenson engineered the line, but it had to be improved considerably by George Hudson before steam trains could use it. The line was closed in 1964, then reopened by dedicated railway enthusiasts, and is now an immensely popular tourist attraction. Scenes from the line feature regularly in films and television, including the popular TV series 'Heartbeat'.

WALK 6
Hutton-le-Hole, Lastingham, Cropton and Appleton-le-Moors

Distance	16km (10 miles)
Start/finish	Ryedale Folk Museum, Hutton-le-Hole, GR 705900
Maps	OS Landranger 94 or 100; OS Explorers OL26 and 27 South
Terrain	Easy walking along low-level paths, tracks and roads, brushing moorland slopes first, then returning through fields later
Refreshments	Pubs and tea shops at Hutton-le-Hole, pubs at Lastingham, Cropton and Appleton-le-Moors
Transport	Regular Moorsbus services to Hutton-le-Hole from Pickering, Helmsley and Danby; Cropton and Appleton-le-Moors have occasional Moorsbus and Hutchinsons bus services; Lastingham has occasional Hutchinsons bus services from Pickering

The three little villages of Hutton-le-Hole, Lastingham and Cropton sit where the Tabular Hills give way to the High Moors. True to form the Tabular Hills display a series of high 'nabs' before the higher moors stretch their uniform heather slopes northwards. This walk links all three villages, then uses the course of the waymarked Tabular Hills Walk to take in a fourth village, Appleton-le-Moors, on the way back to Hutton-le-Hole. Each village has at least a pub offering food and drink, so this is an ideal walk for those who like to be pampered.

Leave the Ryedale Folk Museum in **Hutton-le-Hole** and walk down the road a short way to the **village hall**. Across the road from the hall is a public footpath sign beside a small gate. Follow this path across fields as marked, then cross a footbridge over **Loskey Beck**. Follow a woodland path up through a gate and continue along a grassy track to reach a road. Turn right along the road, then well before reaching a road junction, watch for a public footpath sign pointing left along a grassy track. Follow the track through a gate, noting that some stretches are wet and muddy, then swing right and continue alongside a fence. Cut across a grassy slope as marked, well above **Camomile Farm**. Drop down into a valley where the ground is wet enough to support bog myrtle. Climb up the other side alongside a wall to reach a clear track above the village of **Lastingham**, beside its millennium stone.

LASTINGHAM

This little village is huddled between the Tabular Hills and High Moors and can easily be explored by making a detour from the route. Of particular interest is St Mary's Church, with its Norman crypt and Shrine of St Cedd, originally built in 1078 on the site of an ancient Celtic monastery. Food and drink are available from the Blacksmith's Arms and Lastingham Grange Hotel.

Walk past the millennium stone and follow a sandy track signposted for Hartoft. This quickly becomes a broad grassy track running alongside a drystone wall. It rises gently uphill, then runs downhill, with moorland to the left and fields to the right, eventually fording **Tranmire Beck**. Head straight uphill to a corner of a wall and follow the wall onwards, using a narrower grassy path to reach a clear farm track at **Askew**. Turn right to walk down the track, which becomes a narrow tarmac road leading to a road junction.

Turn left as signposted along a public footpath at the junction, over a step-stile, down a field, turning right alongside the **River Seven**. Cross a step-stile onto a road and turn left across a bridge. Follow the road away from the river, up past **Beckhouse Farm**, then down to a junction. Turn right over another bridge and walk up the road towards **Cropton**. Either walk all the way up the road to reach the village and its pub, or omit the village and turn right along a clear track signposted as the Tabular Hills Walk.

CROPTON

A motte and bailey was built at Cropton in the 12th century, but it was in ruins by the end of the 14th century. St Gregory's Church may have been built on a Norman chapel site, but while it retains its 12th-century font, the building is essentially a 19th-century restoration. The New Inn offers accommodation, food and drink, as well as tours of its micro-brewery. There are other lodgings available around the village too.

The Tabular Hills Walk follows a clear track, but when this track suddenly turns right, leave it by walking straight ahead to enjoy a fine, garlic-scented woodland path along **Mill Bank**. Eventually, at a junction of paths turn right down to the River Seven and cross it using a footbridge. Follow the nearby farm access road uphill, away from **Appleton Mill Farm**, and continue along Hamley Lane. Turn left at a road junction

beside the stump of an old stone cross to approach **Appleton-le-Moors**. The route actually turns right just as it reaches **Dweldapilton Hall** on the outskirts of the village.

APPLETON-LE-MOORS

Appleton is a typical Yorkshire 'croft and toft' village. The 'crofts' are the little cottages arranged on either side of the long main street, the 'tofts' are the pieces of land extending from the back of each dwelling where householders would grow their own vegetables. Imposing Dweldapilton Hall was built by a wealthy whaler. The Moors Inn offers food, drink and accommodation.

Follow the track away from **the hall**, passing the village **sports field**, to reach a prominent junction of tracks. Turn right through a gate and follow an unenclosed track gently uphill through fields. Turn left at another prominent junction of tracks, as marked, along **Lingmoor Lane**. Walk through a gate, then into a wood at another gate. Turn right to walk around the inside edge of the wood, then continue through fields. Turn right along another clear track, called **Bottomfields Lane**,

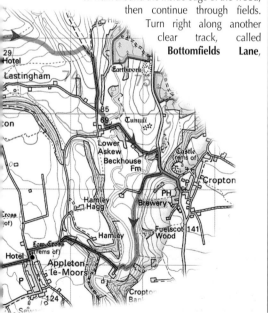

rising gently. Turn left at the top and continue through more fields. The track then drops, steep and narrow, down to a road. Turn right to walk back up into the charming village of **Hutton-le-Hole**.

HUTTON-LE-HOLE

Hutton-le-Hole has a long history of settlement dating back to Neolithic times. The village was mentioned in the Domesday Book as 'Hoton', but throughout the ages it has also been rendered as 'Hege-Hoton', 'Hoton under Heg' and 'Hewton'. As a placename Hutton-le-Hole dates only from the 19th century. The village features the Ryedale Folk Museum, Barn Hotel, Crown Inn and a couple of tea shops and gift shops.

RYEDALE FOLK MUSEUM

Trace the history of Yorkshire folk from 4000 BC to 1953, with plenty of hands-on exhibits, as you wander from one part of the museum site to another. Over a dozen buildings have been erected since 1964, some with roofs supported by enormous cruck frames (curved timbers), some standing in isolation, while others are arranged as a row of small shops. Vintage vehicles, including motorised and horse-drawn carriages, are preserved. Land around the site sprouts vegetables and flowers, including many varieties of cornfield flowers. Local folk often give demonstrations of traditional crafts while wearing period dress. There is an entrance charge, and the museum incorporates a shop, toilets and tourist information centre, ☎ 01751 417367.

Sheep regularly graze the extensive green in the middle of Hutton-le-Hole

WALK 7
Gillamoor, Boonhill Common and Fadmoor

Distance	8km (5 miles)
Start/finish	Royal Oak, Gillamoor, GR 682899
Maps	OS Landranger 94 or 100; OS Explorer OL26 South
Terrain	Easy walking along woodland and field paths with linking roads
Refreshments	Royal Oak at Gillamoor and Plough Inn at Fadmoor
Transport	Occasional Moorsbus and Hutchinsons bus services to Gillamoor and Fadmoor from Helmsley and Pickering

Gillamoor and Fadmoor are quiet, charming little villages with neat greens, a pub apiece and several stone farms and cottages. Both villages are surrounded by fields which rise gradually to Boonhill Common. This common is another of the 'nabs' on the Tabular Hills beyond which stretch extensive heather moorlands. Despite being flanked by the River Dove and Hodge Beck, Gillamoor and Fadmoor were in most respects 'dry' villages, without a constant supply of water. This problem was overcome when lengthy 'leats' were constructed to channel water to both villages from distant sources.

Start from the Royal Oak in **Gillamoor** and walk through the village to reach **St Aidan's Church**. The road runs left of the church and reaches the **Surprise View** which overlooks the River Dove and Spaunton Moor. As the road bends left, branch left along a signposted footpath that runs along the inside edge of a woodland at the top of a steep brow. The path continues alongside a field, then heads straight for a minor road. Turn right to follow the road past a junction, as signposted for Bransdale, beside **Dial Farm**. Walk down a wooded road which levels out among fields and passes **Grays farm**. Turn left along a narrow road marked 'No through road' and

49

The Surprise View at Gillamoor stretches across Farndale to Spaunton Moor

follow it around the lower slopes of **Boonhill Common**, heading downhill a short way.

Head left from the road to follow a signposted bridleway that is initially a grassy track running down past a gate. Walk up through another gate to enter fields, and look back to admire the fine house at **Stonely Woods**. Walk alongside fields and fences, going through gates as marked, to land on another narrow road above **Cherry Tree Farm**. Turn left to cross a cattle-grid and walk past a farm at **Aumery Park**. Just as you leave the last building, turn left up through a gate and walk alongside a fence as signposted for Fadmoor. The fence leads up across a wooded slope, and the path continues across a higher wooded slope with tangled brambly ground cover. Watch out for a step-stile at the top of **the Brow**, leading out into fields on the left.

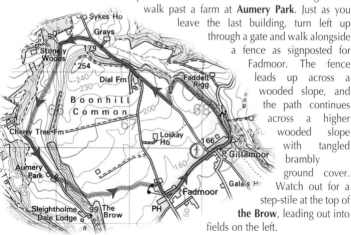

50

GILLAMOOR AND FADMOOR

These two charming little villages lacked a reliable water supply until the 18th century. Joseph Foord engineered a lengthy aqueduct, or 'leat', tapping into distant sources of water to channel a supply to the villages. This supply was still used even into the 20th century, until it was replaced by piped water. The Royal Oak offers food, drink and accommodation in Gillamoor, where there is also a shop. Fadmoor's Plough Inn offers food and drink.

Walk diagonally across the fields, and if no trodden path can be discerned, look ahead to spot the required step-stiles and take note of the direction given by marker arrows at each one. When a road is reached at some farm buildings turn right to walk into the village of **Fadmoor**, then left to cross the central green to leave the village, or visit the Plough Inn for a break. The road continues straight ahead to return to **Gillamoor**.

A little cottage standing beside the broad central green in the village of Fadmoor

WALK 8
Newgate Bank, Rievaulx Moor and Helmsley Bank

Distance	18km (11 miles)
Start/finish	Newgate Bank forest car park, GR 564890
Maps	OS Landranger 100; OS Explorer OL26 South
Terrain	Good forest and moorland tracks giving way to farm tracks and field paths, with some vague forest paths needing careful route-finding
Refreshments	None on the route, but plenty of pubs, cafés and restaurants at nearby Helmsley
Transport	Regular Moorsbus services pass Newgate Bank between Helmsley and Bilsdale

The Tabular Hills rise so high and heathery on Rievaulx Moor and Helmsley Bank that they seem to challenge the wide moorland expanses further north. On a clear day, extensive views can be enjoyed from the high brow of Helmsley Bank, though on this walk views are lost when the route descends into dense forest. After traversing high above wooded Riccal Dale, the walk crosses forested Ash Dale and Beck Dale. Careful route-finding is required along a rather vague and indistinct forest path before clear farm tracks and roads complete the circuit.

The Forestry Commission car park, off the B1257 at **Newgate Bank**, has toilets and access to a viewing platform, but there are no other facilities on or near this walk. Just as the forest access road leaves the main road, a footpath signpost points straight along a clear forest track. Follow it, noting the ground cover of bilberry and brambles. Leave the forest and continue along the track with forest to the left and the heather expanse of **Rievaulx Moor** to the right.

Two trees seen in silhouette on Rievaulx Moor on the way up to Helmsley Bank

The clear track rises gradually, offering fine views of Bilsdale and the high moors on either side of it, with the Cleveland Hills clustered around the dalehead. Pass a trig point at 328m (1076ft) on **Helmsley Bank** and continue gently down the track to cross a minor road. Benches are available at a viewpoint, offering an extensive vista northwards across the High Moors.

Keep walking onwards, following another track gently downhill along the brow. There are only views for a short while before the track runs deep into a forest, where there is a mixture of tree species and the walking is pleasant. Stay always on the clearest track while heading gently downhill, but keep an eye open to spot a couple of viewpoint benches off to the left, overlooking the High Moors, Birk Nab and Riccal Dale from **Cowhouse Bank**.

The track reaches a car park and road. Walk across the road, and a little to the left, to find a barrier gate and a grassy forest path leading onwards. While this isn't actually a right of way, it is in regular use by walkers and horse-riders. Follow it onwards, with glimpses of **Riccal Dale** down to the left. Avoid a right turn, but keep right soon afterwards to follow a muddy track gently down into denser forest. This track swings right from the forest and runs along the edge, where it is firm and grassy, with views across the fields surrounding **Carlton Park Farm**.

Cross a road to see a public footpath sign pointing along a gravel track for **Carlton Grange**, which offers farmhouse bed and breakfast. Walk straight past the house, then cross a step-stile and turn left as marked alongside a field. Turn right and cross another step-stile, then veer right down a grassy track into **Ash Dale**. (Do not follow the track accompanying a power line across the dale.) Notice the fine straight pines in the dale. Climb up the other side and follow a track to **High Baxton's Farm**. Turn left down a road and walk a field's length, then turn right through a gate, signposted as a public footpath, to leave the road.

Walk alongside a field and turn right, then turn left across a step-stile and walk alongside another field. Go through a gate and walk to the corner of the next field. Go through a little gate and cross a forest track, veering slightly right, to pick up and follow a path downhill to the left. This is clear and obvious, surfaced with soft pine needles. It leads down into jungle-like **Beck Dale**, where you cross a stream bed that is normally dry. Climb steeply uphill, then follow a rather narrow and vague path marked by occasional yellow markers – rather like lollipop sticks – on trees. Cross over a **forest track**.

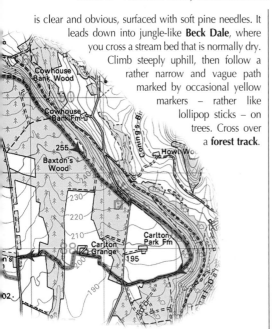

Take great care following the next stretch of the path, and watch carefully to spot evidence of a trodden path, as well as for more of the yellow markers on trees. Cross a **grassy track** and keep walking onwards, taking a more meandering course than the map admits, to reach yet another **grassy track**. Turn right up this track, then left at a junction to follow a clearer track. This can be wet and muddy in places, but stick with it to reach a gate and leave the forest. Follow a grassy track alongside fields, crossing a dip to reach **Oscar Park Farm**. Go through the farmyard and follow the access track to the main **B1257**. Turn right to follow the road, which has a wide grassy verge, and either walk all the way back to **Newgate Bank**, or flag down the Moorsbus if you are on the road when it happens to pass.

WALK 9
Helmsley, Beck Dale and Ash Dale

Distance	11km (6.5 miles)
Start/finish	Market place, Helmsley, GR 612838
Maps	OS Landranger 100; OS Explorer OL26 South
Terrain	Easy woodland tracks and paths through the dales linked by field paths over higher ground
Refreshments	Plenty of pubs, restaurants and cafés around Helmsley
Transport	Helmsley is an important Moorsbus hub with regular services to and from the surrounding countryside; Scarborough & District buses run regularly to and from Scarborough; Hutchinsons buses occasionally serve nearby towns and villages, while Stephensons buses link Helmsley with York

Beck Dale and Ash Dale are on the very doorstep of the bustling market town of Helmsley, yet hardly any of the visitors seem aware of them. These are steep-sided forested dales, cut into the Tabular Hills. Beck Dale is indeed drained by a little beck, while Ash Dale is generally dry. Both dales were essentially carved by torrents of glacial melt-water, and any water they carry today is a mere trickle compared to their past burden. Both dales are easily accessed from Helmsley, and run parallel throughout their length. They are also easily linked using field paths from one to the other.

Start at the **market place** in the middle of **Helmsley** and follow the Stokesley road out of town. This leads along **Church Street** past All Saints Church, then along **High Street**, which has a beck running along its length. Keep on the right-hand side of the road, but avoid a turning marked as a private road. Turn right a little later, as signposted along a footpath, to follow a stone-paved path alongside a beck. Cross a little **footbridge** and continue upstream, soon following a clear track towards a former **sawmill** site.

Keep following the track, which runs along the grassy floor of wooded **Beck Dale**. When a junction of tracks is reached, turn right as signposted along a footpath. Go through a pheasant enclosure and later follow the track as it crosses the beck. Look out for squirrels and deer, as well as woodland birds. The track fords the beck three times in quick succession before running out of room altogether on the floor of the dale. The track climbs up the valley side and is signposted as a footpath. At a higher level turn left, also signposted as a footpath. Don't follow a clear grassy track, but head up a narrow path through conifers. This path soon runs across a more open forested brow with a ground cover of bracken and brambles.

Turn right along a track, then quickly right again through a little gate, followed by a left turn alongside a field. Go through a gate and walk alongside another field, cross a stile, then turn right and then left alongside the field to reach a road. Turn right along the road, away from **High Baxton's Farm**, for the space of one large field. Turn left off the road to follow a clear track down into wooded **Ash Dale**. Turn right to walk down along the grassy floor of the valley, signposted for Helmsley, with steep wooded slopes on either side. There is no way of gauging progress down the dale, but when the steep bank on the right dwindles to nothing, watch for a narrow path slipping out of the woods through a gate on that side. Walk alongside a field and go through a gate. Turn right through fields to reach another gate, then turn left. Turn right round the field and left at another gate.

THE NORTH YORK MOORS

Helmsley Castle keep was reduced to a ruin by Cromwellian forces

Walk between sports pitches and continue into **Helmsley** via Warwick Place. Turn right and left by road, then walk through the churchyard to finish back on the **market place**.

HELMSLEY

Helmsley is a quintessential Yorkshire market town, tracing its ancestry back to Anglo-Saxon times. The spacious market place fills with stalls on market day and serves as a car park at other times. Apart from the market cross, there is a towering monument to the second Lord Feversham. Stout stone buildings stand on all sides of the market place, and a couple of poky alleys lined with quaint little shops lead away. The most prominent building is the town hall. All Saints Church was founded in Norman times, but is essentially a 19th-century structure. There is a good range of accommodation, banks with ATMs, a post office, toilets, plenty of pubs, restaurants and tea rooms, as well as shops galore, including an outdoor gear store. The tourist information centre is in the town hall in the market place, ☎ 01439 770173.

HELMSLEY CASTLE

Not every visitor to Helmsley is aware of Helmsley Castle, despite its proximity to the town centre. It was built around 1200 and saw plenty of strife in 1644, during the Civil War. Colonel Crosland held the castle for the Crown, while Sir Thomas Fairfax led the besieging Parliamentarian force. Fairfax was hit by a musket ball during one assault, and his siege was threatened by a Royalist relief force from Knaresborough Castle. The relief force was eventually beaten back and harried as far as Black Hambleton. The castle surrendered towards the end of 1644 and was rendered useless during 1646 and 1647 when parts of the keep and walls were destroyed. There is an entrance charge, ☎ 01439 770442.

DUNCOMBE PARK

Another fine attraction near Helmsley is Duncombe Park, home of Lord Feversham. Visitors are charged according to whether they just wish to roam and explore the extensive Arcadian parkland, or include the garden and terraces, or embark on a guided tour of the large house at the centre of the park. There is also a tea room and a thriving events calendar. ☎ 01439 770213.

WALK 10
Hawnby Hill and Easterside Hill

Distance	7.5km (4.5 miles)
Start/finish	Hawnby Hotel, Hawnby, GR 542898
Maps	OS Landranger 100; OS Explorer OL26 South
Terrain	A short but sometimes difficult walk as paths can be steep and rugged – they are clear at first, but later covered in bracken
Refreshments	Hawnby Hotel in the village of Hawnby
Transport	None to Hawnby, but regular Moorsbus services between Helmsley and Bilsdale pass Laskill, which is close to Easterside Hill

Rising from the confluence of Ryedale and Bilsdale, Hawnby Hill and Easterside Hill are twins with a striking appearance, flanked by gentle dales and softly sloping heather moors. But for the fact that they sit lower than the surrounding moorlands, they would command attention from afar, but despite their steep slopes and shapely form, visitors tend to notice them only at close quarters. This walk uses new access paths to traverse the crest of Hawnby Hill and climb near the summit of Easterside Hill in a fine, short circular walk from the charming little village of Hawnby.

Hawnby is only a small village and the **Hawnby Hotel** stands at a road junction from where a public footpath is signposted uphill. Climb up an old lane to reach a gate where paths are marked left and right. Take the left one, but not up to the step-stile as marked. Instead, go a little further uphill to a small gate in the top corner of a field. Go through the gate and follow a narrow path that swings right and climbs steeply up a slope of bracken. It becomes a clear grassy path climbing onto the crest of **Hawnby Hill**. The summit cairn is reached at 294m (965ft), and there are extensive views across Ryedale to Black Hambleton, across Bilsdale Moor and Bransdale

Moor, to neighbouring Easterside Hill, and the distant Yorkshire Wolds.

Continue along a sharper part of the crest where a bouldery limestone scree falls to the left. Keep straight ahead along the ridge, then zigzag down the steep end of the hill, aiming for a cattle-grid on a road at **Moor Gate**. Cross the grid and turn right along a gravel access road across a moorland slope.

The striking profile of Hawnby Hill as seen from the upper part of Ryedale

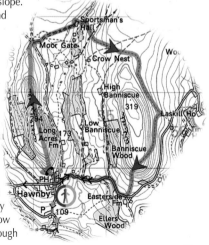

Go down to **Sportsman's Hall** and reach the end of the track. Turn left, as marked, across a muddy field, before turning right down to a gate. Drop down a wooded slope and cross a footbridge over **Ladhill Beck**.

The path leading uphill is vague in places, so look out for blobs of yellow paint on boulders. Cross a grassy track on the heather and bilberry slope and go over a **stone step-stile** at the top corner of a wall. Continue across the heather moor as marked by paint blobs and small cairns. Follow a wall onwards and forge through

The view across country towards Bilsdale Moor as seen from Hawnby Hill

bracken as the wall turns right across a slope. Watch carefully for a waymark arrow on the right, pointing uphill to indicate an old path on the hillside. Follow this faithfully uphill, and follow posts across the higher slopes of **Easterside Hill**, over 280m (920ft). Watch for more posts and markers on the descent, then cross a field to land on a minor road at **Easterside Farm bed and breakfast**. Turn right to follow the road downhill, then more steeply downhill to cross **Ladhill Beck**. A steep climb up the road is followed by a left turn at the top to return to the village of **Hawnby**.

THE HAMBLETON HILLS

Geologically the Hambleton Hills are an extension of the Tabular Hills, separated from them by Ryedale, and with a character all of their own. Essentially the Hambleton Hills rise gently from the dales within the North York Moors National Park, then drop precipitously to the plains. Indeed, some of the slopes are not only steep, but excessively steep, and even vertical cliff edges. Despite having the appearance of an inaccessible rampart, these cliffs are breached by a busy main road along which many visitors find their way into the national park. In order to catch visitors at an appropriate point, the national park authority constructed a visitor centre on Sutton Bank at the top of the road.

Many walkers have come to know and love the Hambleton Hills by setting off along the waymarked Cleveland Way, one of Britain's national trails. This route leads from Helmsley to Rievaulx, then climbs gradually from the dales via the village of Cold Kirby to reach Sutton Bank. At that point walkers are faced with a choice of routes, as there is a diversion to see the celebrated Kilburn White Horse, which was carved into the steep slopes in the 19th century. However, it is the cliff-edge walk that is the most memorable feature of these hills, and when the cliffs finally give way to mere hillsides, the course of the ancient Hambleton Drove Road is another abiding feature. This long straight track soars over the moors, almost reaching the summit of Black Hambleton itself.

There is no doubt that by the time walkers experience the broad heather slopes of Black Hambleton, comparisons with the High Moors in the central parts of the national park are inevitable. Black Hambleton is both high and heathery enough to rival most of the broad bleak moors at the heart of the North York Moors, and many walkers crossing its flanks will find themselves yearning for more of the same.

Four walks in the Hambleton Hills are described, showing off something of the variety of landscapes in this little limestone upland. Rievaulx Abbey and Byland Abbey are visited on separate walks and have obvious monastic links. The splendid cliff-edge walk from Sutton Bank is complemented by an exploration of the lower slopes around curious Gormire Lake. A longer walk takes in a few villages before heading for the high and wild slopes of Black Hambleton, by which time the High Moors and Cleveland Hills begin to dominate onward views and altogether tougher walks begin to beckon.

WALK 11
Rievaulx Abbey and Old Byland

Distance	12km (7.5 miles)
Start/finish	Rievaulx Abbey, GR 574848
Maps	OS Landranger 100; OS Explorer OL26 South
Terrain	Generally easy walking along minor roads, clear tracks and paths, though some paths can be a bit overgrown or muddy
Refreshments	None on the route, but plenty of pubs, restaurants and cafés in nearby Helmsley
Transport	Occasional Moorsbus services to Rievaulx from Helmsley, with regular services passing Rievaulx Terrace above the village and abbey

Rievaulx Abbey is a remarkable sight, its stout soaring columns and elegant arches dominating the small stone village of Rievaulx. Naturally the abbey attracts a lot of visitors, and the nearby Cleveland Way is quite popular too, but some of the other paths and tracks in the area, such as those around the village of Old Byland, are much quieter. This walk is essentially confined to wooded dales, except when it crosses higher fields to get from one dale to another. Allow extra time if exploring Rievaulx Abbey or Rievaulx Terrace.

Start at **Rievaulx Abbey**, either exploring the site straight away or taking note of its opening times for later in the day. Toilets are available, and parking for patrons, though parking is tight around Rievaulx and it makes sense to use the Moorsbus for access. Walk along a road beside the River Rye to reach **Rievaulx Bridge**. Turn right to cross it and walk straight ahead to pass a road junction, following the road signposted for Scawton until a clear gravel track on the right is marked as the Cleveland Way.

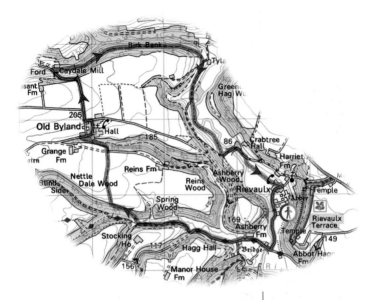

The track runs alongside a wood and passes a few shallow **fishing ponds**, then the route crosses stepping stones on the right. Go through a small gate, cross a track, cross a step-stile, cross a small field and cross a footbridge – all in that order. Turn left uphill through **Nettle Dale Wood** and keep to the trodden path climbing gradually uphill (not along the one branching left). Emerge to walk alongside fields and go through gates, crossing a track, before going through another gate into a wood. Turn left along a path lined with nettles and brambles to pass through a little **wooded dale**, gradually crossing the valley before being drawn up to a small gate. Step onto a road and turn right to enter the village of **Old Byland**, following the road as it swings left to reach the sloping green surrounded by old stone houses.

Walk to the top end of the village and turn left as signposted for 'Hawnby' and 'Boltby', then turn right at a junction. Walk straight along a narrow road marked as

OLD BYLAND

The village of Old Byland is indeed old, having been mentioned in the Domesday Book as 'Begesland'. There was a wooden church there at the time, but there may have been a stone church on the site previously. The land around Old Byland was granted to Savignian monks in 1142, and they basically laid out the village in its current form. They left soon afterwards, in 1147, to build Byland Abbey (see Walk 12). Visitors would miss All Saints Church if it wasn't signposted, and careful study of its stonework reveals some interesting Norman carvings.

leading to a ford. The road swings left and drops into Caydale, overlooking **Caydale Mill**. Before reaching the bottom of the road watch for a sharp right turn at a gate signposted as a public bridleway. Follow a grassy path across a flowery grassy slope. The path runs almost down to a river, then rises to enter a coppice woodland. The path in the woods can be quite muddy, and it later runs past a **stand of conifers**. Continue back into deciduous woodland as the path drops gradually downhill. Go through a gate and along a grassy track, then through another gate onto a tarmac farm road near **Tylas Farm**.

Turn right along the road and follow it down into a dip. Turn left to leave the road at a gate and follow a clear path through a field. Continue along a duckboard path on a wooded slope above the **River Rye**. Cross a

RIEVAULX ABBEY

Founded in 1132 by Walter l'Espec, Rievaulx Abbey was a Cistercian house and once the home of St Aelred. During its construction a short canal was built and rafts bore blocks of stone to the site. The abbey is built almost on a north–south axis, rather than the usual east–west, because of its situation in a rather narrow dale. Only 35 years after its foundation the abbey boasted 140 monks, 250 lay brothers and 260 hired laymen. Even in its ruinous state the walls rise to a prodigious height and give a good impression of the size and complexity of the building. There is an entrance charge, ☎ 01439 798228.

stile and continue across a rough strip of land to reach a track. Turn left to follow the track over the fine stone arch of **Bow Bridge**. Walk uphill until there is a footpath sign-post and a small gate on the right. Follow a riverside path downstream as marked. Note, when veering away from the river later, that the muddy ditch off to the left is an old canal, once used to float stone to Rievaulx Abbey during its construction. Keep going through gates to reach a road in the village of **Rievaulx**, and turn right to return to the abbey.

An optional short extension involves turning left along the road in **Rievaulx** and walking through the village to pass the church. Here, look out on the right for a path winding up a wooded slope to **Rievaulx Terrace and Temples**, a National Trust property.

RIEVAULX TERRACE AND TEMPLES

The grassy brow of Rievaulx Terrace offers fine views and a short extension to the day's walk. There are two classical temples, the Tuscan Temple and the Ionic Temple, to visit. Both were built in the 18th century and the Ionic Temple features splendid paintings on its ceiling. There is an entrance charge, ☎ 01439 798340.

WALK 12
Byland Abbey, Mount Snever and Oldstead

Distance	8km (5 miles)
Start/finish	Abbey Inn, Byland Abbey, GR 548789
Maps	OS Landranger 100; OS Explorer OL26 South
Terrain	Easy walking along woodland paths, field paths and farm tracks
Refreshments	Abbey Inn at Byland Abbey, Wombwell Arms at Wass, Black Swan Inn at Oldstead
Transport	Stephenson's buses serve Byland Abbey from Helmsley and York, and there are occasional Moorsbus services from Helmsley

Byland Abbey's west wall is an outstanding feature that is seen in many pictorial compilations of scenes from the North York Moors. The top half of its round window has collapsed, leaving two horns of masonry pointing to the sky. The nearby villages of Wass and Oldstead are pretty, but lack any outstanding features, though both have pubs. Mount Snever is no more than a wooded hill, and the Mount Snever Observatory is a curious viewpoint tower. However, a gentle circular walk taking in all these places opens up a quiet and interesting part of the national park to visitors.

Start at the Abbey Inn and admire **Byland Abbey**. Follow the road signposted for Wass, then turn left along the **Abbey House** access road. Don't walk to the house, but turn right and cross stiles through fields, bearing a little to the left uphill to find a small gate. The field path leads to a road just outside the village of **Wass**. Turn left up a battered woodland road, and go straight through a little gate signposted for Cam Farm to follow a grassy path beside a wood. The path climbs to a stile and enters the wood at a pronounced bend on a track. Head left as

signposted again for Cam Farm. The track is flanked by **pheasant enclosures** and dips downhill, then rises, then swings sharp left. Keep right at this point, in effect walking straight ahead, to follow another track. As this track climbs it can be a bit muddy, and it narrows to become a brambly path at a higher level around **Elm Hag**.

The ruins of Byland Abbey stretch to the sky and cover a large area of ground

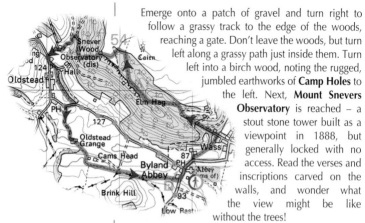

Emerge onto a patch of gravel and turn right to follow a grassy track to the edge of the woods, reaching a gate. Don't leave the woods, but turn left along a grassy path just inside them. Turn left into a birch wood, noting the rugged, jumbled earthworks of **Camp Holes** to the left. Next, **Mount Snevers Observatory** is reached – a stout stone tower built as a viewpoint in 1888, but generally locked with no access. Read the verses and inscriptions carved on the walls, and wonder what the view might be like without the trees!

A path drops steeply from the tower through **Snever Wood**. Follow it all the way down to a track, and turn right to follow the track more gently downhill. Keep left at track junctions to leave the woods and follow a narrow tarmac road downhill. Keep left at road junctions to follow the road just to the first buildings in the village of **Oldstead**. (If you enter the village you will find the Black Swan Inn at the far end.) However, to continue the walk turn left along an access road to pass gate piers, as if heading for **Oldstead Mill**, along a tree-shaded avenue.

A footpath signpost points uphill to the right, then you turn left along the top of a wooded brow. Walk alongside small fields, using stiles and gates, then follow the path down to a minor road. Turn right, as if walking back towards the village of **Oldstead**, but turn left along the access road for **Oldstead Grange**. Pass in front of a farm guesthouse and walk through the farmyard.

Cross a stile beside a gate as marked. Walk down a grassy track into a valley and cross a stile beside a gate at the bottom. Turn left up a narrow path through a tangled belt of woodland. Keep right, and then turn left to follow a field boundary, keeping well clear of the farmhouse at **Cams Head**. Switch to another field boundary as marked and signposted for Byland Abbey to

The Black Swan Inn at Oldstead where a short detour leads to food and drink

continue. The path heads diagonally across a field, then runs alongside an orchard to cross a stile and reach a road. Turn left along the road to return to **Byland Abbey** and the Abbey Inn.

BYLAND ABBEY

After rejecting a site at Old Byland (see Walk 11) the Savignian monks chose to found an abbey here, though they had to drain the land before building in 1177. The ruins of Byland Abbey are quite extensive, but rather dominated by what you see from the roadside. In fact the abbey extended far beyond what you can discern on the ground, and was larger than Rievaulx and Fountains abbeys. A fine spread of decorative floor tiles remain in their original position, and the abbey grounds had fish ponds, a mill and market gardens, so that it was entirely self-sufficient for food. There is an entrance charge, ☎ 01347 868614.

WALK 13
Sutton Bank, Gormire Lake and the White Horse

Distance	15km (9.5 miles)
Start/finish	Visitor centre, Sutton Bank, GR 515830
Maps	OS Landranger 100; OS Explorer OL26 South
Terrain	Generally easy paths along cliff edges, through forest, wood sand fields, with farm and forest tracks too; some paths can be vague in places
Refreshments	Restaurant at the visitor centre on Sutton Bank
Transport	Regular Moorsbus services run to and from Sutton Bank, and Scarborough & District bus services to and from Helmsley and Scarborough

The most dramatic part of the Hambleton Hills is around Sutton Bank, where cliff edges and steep wooded slopes face west towards the plains. The Cleveland Way makes use of the cliff-top paths, but walkers on that route know little of what lies at the foot of the slope. This walk reveals a network of paths and tracks, reaches the shore of Gormire Lake, and wanders past farms and through woods to climb to the Kilburn White Horse. All this is achieved from Sutton Bank, one of the gateways to the North York Moors National Park, where there is an interesting and informative visitor centre.

Leave the visitor centre at **Sutton Bank** and walk as if you are going to follow the busy main **A170** over the edge. However, turn right to follow the path signposted as the Cleveland Way. The path initially runs through patchy woodland around 300m (985ft), with only occasional glimpses over the cliffs to the left. Gormire Lake is seen in a wooded hollow at the foot of **Whitestone Cliff**, with the plains stretching beyond. The cliff path is grassy and gently graded, dropping slightly as it turns right and later swings left. The cliffs ease to become a wooded slope, then there is a gradual ascent towards **Boltby Scar**. You can walk up to the top of the scar, which is the site of an Iron Age hill fort at 330m (1080ft), but our route actually turns left downhill beforehand, signposted as a bridleway to Boltby.

The path runs down a grassy groove, then a gate leads into a forest. Follow a muddy track downhill and cross a forest track. Go through a gate and cross the open space of **Little Moor**. Go through another gate and follow a forest path further downhill. The forest gives way to oak and birch before there are views across lower fields. Turn left and follow a path downhill, just inside the woodland, towards **Greendale**, and go through a gate to approach the farm.

Just before reaching the buildings, turn left as marked by arrows and cross a stile to follow a narrow path up across a slope of bracken. Watch carefully for the line of the path, and more markers, to cross a rough grassy slope between a forest and a wood. Reach a field beyond, where the path is usually mown short, and leave the field through a gate to stay well to the left of **Southwoods Hall**. Go through another gate and swing right alongside the stout stone wall encircling the hall. A bridleway signpost points through a small gate marked with a blue arrow. Join and follow the access road a short way from Southwoods Hall, then walk

A view of Gormire Lake in its wooded hollow from the cliffs around Sutton Bank

parallel to the road as directed to pass the main gate. Walk straight ahead through another gate, as indicated by signposts for Gormire. Go through a gate beside another house and turn left, then swing right into wild woodlands to reach the shore of **Gormire Lake**.

GORMIRE LAKE

This little lake is entirely natural, but unusual, since the area does not readily support lakes. It was formed when a huge section of the escarpment slumped onto the plains, so that the detached strata tilted back at an angle, leaving a small valley between itself and the freshly-broken cliff face. The valley was filled with rubble and clay from the fracture, so that water was able to pool in a hollow, whereas normally it would have seeped into the limestone bedrock. According to local lore the lake is bottomless – in fact it is quite shallow. The surrounding woodlands are home to red, fallow and roe deer, though these are seldom seen.

There is a path signposted straight uphill if anyone wishes to finish early and return to **Sutton Bank**. To stay on the route, follow the low path away from the shore and go through a gate to reach **Gormire Farm**. Turn right into the farmyard, then left to leave through a gate. Continue as marked along a grassy track to another gate. Keep right to walk up through a field and cross a step-stile. Walk down through a field to reach a gate and step-stile giving way to the busy main **A170**. Turn right to walk alongside the road, then cross to reach an old telegraph pole where there is a step-stile in a hedge.

Walk down from the busy road towards **Hood Grange** and keep to the right of the farm buildings. Cross the access road and a small footbridge beyond. Turn left as directed alongside a field, then turn right as signposted up through a big field to enter a forest at a corner. Turn left up a forest track, which later dips downhill a little. Keep straight on at a junction, up and over a forested gap between **Hood Hill** and Roulston Scar. Walk downhill and keep left at a junction to follow a track that climbs through a mixed plantation. Turn right at a junction and contour to reach a barrier gate and minor road. Turn left to climb up the steep winding road, which becomes even steeper before reaching the top of the brow. Turn left along a clear path to reach the celebrated **White Horse**, though it is difficult to see from such close quarters.

KILBURN WHITE HORSE

Only the head of the White Horse can be seen from the path. It was cut in 1857 under the direction of local schoolmaster John Hodgson. The inspiration came from another local man, Thomas Taylor, who had witnessed the cleaning and maintenance of a white horse in the south. As the bedrock is oolitic limestone, rather than white chalk, the Kilburn White Horse needs occasional applications of whitewash. The figure measures 96m (314ft) by 69m (228ft) and is a landmark for many on the lower plains. Of greater antiquity, cutting across a nearby glider field, is the Casten Dike, which may have once formed a defensive or territorial boundary on the promontory.

The view back along the cliffs from Sutton Bank at the end of the walk

Follow a clear path along a cliff edge of **Roulston Scar**, around 290m (950ft). There is a glider field here and you should heed the warning signs: Do not short cut across the airfield, watch out for low-flying gliders and do not tamper with towing cables. Later, pass a three-fingered signpost for the Cleveland Way, and stay on the clearest cliff-edge path as signposted for **Sutton Bank**. (Author James Herriot had a special affection for the view from here.) Cross the busy A170 and keep to the right, through a car park, to return to the visitor centre.

NATIONAL PARK VISITOR CENTRE

The North York Moors National Park Visitor Centre catches tourists at one of the busiest entry points for the national park. Displays and exhibits focus on conservation in order to encourage sensitive and thoughtful recreation. Maps and guides are on sale, and there is a restaurant and toilets on site. Regular Moorsbus services run from the centre, to encourage visitors to leave their cars behind. To check opening times ☎ 01845 597426.

WALK 14
Osmotherley, Thimbleby, Siltons and Black Hambleton

Distance	19km (12 miles)
Start/finish	Market cross, Osmotherley, GR 456972
Maps	OS Landrangers 99 and 100; OS Explorer OL26 South
Terrain	Generally easy, but a long walk – field paths, forest tracks, minor roads and farm tracks, followed by a high moorland track later in the day
Refreshments	Queen Catherine Hotel and tea rooms in Osmotherley, Gold Cup Inn at Nether Silton
Transport	Regular Abbott's bus services to Osmotherley from Northallerton and Stokesley; occasional Moorsbus services to Osmotherley from Stokesley and Guisborough

The Hambleton Hills reach their highest and proudest moment on Black Hambleton – a moorland crest so wild and heathery that it rivals the High Moors stretching westwards. The Hambleton Drove Road has long been regarded as a classic route over the broad moorland top, and the Cleveland Way makes good use of it between Sutton Bank and Osmotherley. Few walkers know their way around the lower slopes, yet there are lovely little villages that can be linked with roads, tracks and paths, as well as forests, fields and farms to explore. All this can be achieved on the following walk.

Start at the market cross in **Osmotherley** and follow the Stokesley road a short way. Turn left along **School Lane** and go straight down a narrow enclosed path, continuing straight down a field where trees create a 'low-headroom' situation! Go through a gate at the bottom and turn right along a track. This becomes grassy, then you cross a metal footbridge over **Cod Beck**. Walk through a field and cross an access track, then pass little sports pitches to reach a minor road. Turn right along the road, up into the village of **Thimbleby** and out at the other side.

Turn left where an old sign says 'Bridle Road and Footpath to Siltons'. Walk up a broad clear track and go into a forest. Turn right as signposted bridleway, then at a fork head up to the left as signposted bridleway again. Follow the forest track uphill, crossing bare rock at times, before it swings left at the top, around 230m (755ft). Turn right down a narrow woodland path which is steep and runs through a slippery runnel before landing on a narrow road. Turn right to follow the road down into the village of **Over Silton**.

Turn left at a junction and follow the road signposted for Nether Silton. Watch out for a gate, stile and bridleway signpost on the right. Walk down through a field, through a gate and across a beck. Walk up to **Greystone Farm** and leave along its access track. Turn left up a road into **Nether Silton**, passing its sloping green and the Gold Cup Inn. Follow the road up out of the village, then downhill as signposted for Kepwick. The huge bulk of Black Hambleton rises to the left and will be reached in due course, but first cross a bridge at the bottom of the road, then follow the road uphill and turn left to reach **Cross Lodge**.

Turn left at the lodge to follow a farm access road uphill. This passes between a pine-clad hill and a wooded valley. Keep to the right of the buildings at **Nab Farm** to follow a clear track onwards. This swings right to cross a stream, then you turn left up through a gate in a wall. An obvious grassy path leads up a bracken slope onto heathery **Kepwick Moor**, then follows a drystone wall over a grassy moor to reach a gate. Go through the gate to find more heather and turn left to follow **Hambleton** Drove Road.

HAMBLETON DROVE ROAD

This ancient drove road may have been based on a prehistoric ridgeway. Travellers and traders would have found it easier to traverse the high ground than risk passage through the plains, which were densely wooded, swampy in places, and inhabited by wild animals. Even long after the lowlands were tamed, cattle drovers used the high ground to avoid enclosed farmland and expensive turnpikes. Drovers covered immense distances, moving livestock from Scotland to London for a good price when stock was scarce around the capital. The 18th and 19th centuries saw brisk trade, with herds of up to 1000 on the move. As drovers could be charged 1*s*/6*d* (7.5 pence) per score of cattle on a turnpike, great savings were made by avoiding them!

A view of the little reservoir and surrounding woodlands in Oak Dale

Turn left along a broad, velvet-green track with a wall to the left. Go through a gate onto a heather moor and enjoy views across to the distant Yorkshire Dales. The track reaches a gate and cattle-grid and turns left at **Whitestones**, still with heather moorland to the right and a drystone wall to the left, but the surface is now stonier, running at around 390m (1280ft). Pass a cairn on the slopes of **Black Hambleton** and descend a rugged track in a groove beside the forest – there are views ahead of Osmotherley. The track becomes better surfaced and leads away from the forest onto the grass and heather slopes of **Thimbleby Moor**. Go through a gate and reach a corner of a road at a small car park at **Square Corner**.

Turn left down a gravel path that becomes a stone-paved path, dropping down a bracken slope into woods. Cross a footbridge and walk along a track beside a **reservoir**. Follow the reservoir access road past a house called **Oak Dale**, heading downhill before climbing uphill through woods. Turn left down a minor road, then right up a track. Turn left downhill, towards **White House** as signposted Cleveland Way, but keep well to the right of the house, as marked. Drop down through fields into a wooded valley to cross a **footbridge**, then climb up steps on a wooded slope. Follow a clear path through fields, squeezing between gardens and houses as marked, then through an alleyway to pop out into the middle of **Osmotherley** and end back at the **market cross**.

THE CLEVELAND HILLS

The Cleveland Hills are memorable for their shapely forms and steepness. In a sense they are simply a continuation of the west-facing scarp that looks out from the North York Moors to the level plains. However, the scarp slope is cut deeply by rugged gaps and valleys that leave outstanding little hills with fairly distinctive shapes, quite unlike the rolling tablelands and moorlands that are common in other parts of the national park. In effect, walkers traversing this little range find themselves on a monstrous roller coaster, climbing steeply uphill, enjoying high-level promenades, then dropping precipitately to rugged gaps between the hills, over and over again.

The underlying rocks in this range are essentially from the lower and middle Jurassic period, some 170–200 million years old. The lower beds include Lias shales and ironstones, which have been extensively quarried, while the neighbouring High Moors are generally capped by sandstones from the Ravenscar group, which is why the moorlands present smoother profiles than the dissected Cleveland Hills at the edge of the North York Moors. Over the past few centuries these hills were hacked and blasted by quarrymen and miners in search of alum shales, ironstone and jet, leaving some slopes looking bare and barren, while other places are covered in rocky rubble.

Over the past few decades the Cleveland Way, Lyke Wake Walk, Coast to Coast Walk and other less well-known routes have been drawn along the crest of the Cleveland Hills, so that countless thousands of walkers have experienced the delights, as well as the rigours, of the full traverse. With the sheer pressure of pounding feet, huge scars were ripped out of the hillsides, so that extensive restoration had to take place. Walkers who remember the days when the hills were scored by trenches full of mud and rubble will now be amazed to find stone-paved paths with re-vegetated margins, which have the potential to last for centuries with a little ongoing care and maintenance.

Five walks are offered in the following pages to enable walkers to explore the Cleveland Hills. One of them is a fairly gentle walk over Beacon Hill from Osmotherley. Two rather more strenuous walks climb into the hills from Chop Gate at the head of Bilsdale. Another two moderate walks explore lesser-known parts of the range from the tiny little village of Kildale. Bear in mind that the course of the Lyke Wake Walk, described towards the end of this guidebook, offers another chance to enjoy an extended day's walk through the Cleveland Hills. The true scale and nature of the range quickly becomes apparent as each splendid hill is climbed in turn, and then you climb another!

WALK 15
Osmotherley, Beacon Hill and High Lane

Distance	13km (8 miles), or 10km (6 miles) without detours
Start/finish	Market cross, Osmotherley, GR 456972
Maps	OS Landrangers 93, 99 and 100; OS Explorer OL26 South and North
Terrain	Generally easy paths and tracks through fields, with some woodland, moorland and short, steep slopes
Refreshments	Pub and tea rooms in Osmotherley, café at Mount Grace Priory, Chequers tea room off-route from High Lane
Transport	Regular Abbott's bus services to Osmotherley from Northallerton and Stokesley; occasional Moorsbus services to Osmotherley from Stokesley and Guisborough

Beacon Hill is the most accessible and gentle of the Cleveland Hills. From its summit there are good views of the bleaker parts of the North York Moors National Park. The hill is easily climbed from Osmotherley, and as this is a short walk, there is scope for making detours to interesting places such as Lady's Chapel and Mount Grace Priory. A fine old track called High Lane is used later, which runs closer to the moors, before a short stretch of the Cleveland Way is used to return straight to Osmotherley.

Leave the market cross in **Osmotherley** by following the road called North End, and turn left at the top of the village as signposted for the Cleveland Way. Follow a stony access road past a few houses, continuing uphill to a fork. **Lady's Chapel** is signposted up to the right and is reached by following a track flanked by the Stations of the Cross.

Walk back down the access track and turn right as signposted for the Cleveland Way to reach **Chapel Wood**

Farm. Turn left to walk through the farmyard, then walk into fields and turn right downhill as directed. Cross a stile at the bottom corner of the fields, then walk down a path through **Mount Grace Wood**. A footbridge finally leads to a car park, where there is access to **Mount Grace Priory** ruins, the Jacobean manor and its lovely gardens.

Retrace your steps back up to **Chapel Wood Farm** and walk through the farmyard before turning left to follow a track through fields to **Arncliffe Wood**. Turn right up a clear path and continue along the inside edge of the wood, following a drystone wall over the crest of the hill. Pass the Telecom station on **Beacon Hill**, as well as a trig point at 299m (981ft). Drop downhill to reach a couple of gates leading onto heathery **Scarth Wood Moor**. Views ahead through the Cleveland Hills lead the eye to the little pyramidal peak of Roseberry Topping, seen far away. A clear gravel or stone-paved path runs down the moorland slope. Turn right at a junction to walk down a track sign-posted as a bridleway – this leads to a minor road at Scarth Nick.

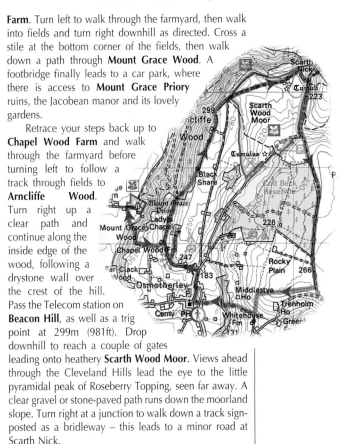

LADY'S CHAPEL

This old chapel, attached to a house and restored from a ruin, is said to have been built in 1515 by Catherine of Aragon, first wife of Henry VIII, for the recluse Thomas Parkinson. A number of miracles are said to have taken place there, and the chapel remains a popular site of pilgrimage.

MOUNT GRACE PRIORY

Mount Grace Priory was a Carthusian monastery founded in 1398 by Thomas de Holand. Of particular interest are the two-storey monks' cells around the cloister, one of which has been restored to its original condition. Each cell had a living room, study, bedroom and small herb garden. The central tower of the priory church remains intact. The ruins stand beside an interesting Jacobean manor, and there are lovely gardens to explore, as well as a café on site. There is an entrance charge, ☎ 01609 883494.

Turn right to walk up the road, crossing its highest part and walking downhill. Turn left across a footbridge by a ford and walk up a steep and rocky track. The rest of this track, called **High Lane**, is gently graded and easy. As the track rises onto **Pamperdale Moor** there is forest to the right and rough pasture enclosures on the left. The highest parts run at 270m (885ft), and the track eventually becomes a tarmac road. (If you keep walking straight ahead and turn left at a road junction, you soon reach the tea rooms at Chequers.) Turn right as signposted along a public footpath and walk along another track on a grassy brow at **Rookhaw**. Views across a valley take in the moorland hump of Black Hambleton.

Cross a stile at the end of the track and walk alongside a field. Walk down alongside another field to reach another track. Turn left and follow the track downhill as it narrows, flanked by bushes. Turn right as signposted for the Cleveland Way. Walk down towards **White House**,

SCARTH NICK

Scarth Nick was cut by glacial melt-water when a torrent poured through a gap in the hills as a stagnant mass of ice melted on the higher ground. The road at Scarth Nick is quite innocuous, but in the 18th century the well-travelled Arthur Young was scathing about it. He said 'The going down into Cleveland is beyond all description terrible ... for you go through such steep, rough, narrow, rocky precipices that I would sincerely advise any friend to go a hundred miles to avoid it.'

but keep well to the right of it as marked. Drop down through fields into a wooded valley to cross a **footbridge**, then climb up steps on a wooded slope. Follow a clear path through fields, squeezing between gardens and houses as marked, then through an alleyway to pop out into the middle of **Osmotherley** and end back at the market cross.

A stone-paved path leads across Scarth Wood Moor towards Scarth Nick

OSMOTHERLEY

Osmotherley was once known as 'Asmundrelac', or 'Asmund's clearing'. It is a charming stone village with a green heart. Three roads meet at the market cross and there is a stone table on five legs where baskets of market produce were sold. John Wesley preached from this stone, and the Methodist chapel in the village has a date-stone of 1754. There is accommodation, a post office, the Queen Catherine pub, a couple of tea rooms and a couple of shops, including the Walking Shop if you need any outdoor gear. Be sure to visit the award-winning toilets and stick a message on the wall!

WALK 16
Chop Gate, Cringle Moor and Cock Howe

Distance	16km (10 miles)
Start/finish	Chop Gate car park, Bilsdale, GR 558993
Maps	OS Landrangers 93 and 100; OS Explorer OL26 South and North
Terrain	A tough walk along firm, clear paths and tracks, though these can be muddy for short stretches; the high moors are exposed in bad weather
Refreshments	Buck Inn at Chop Gate, Lord Stones Café at Carlton Bank
Transport	Regular Moorsbus services run to Chop Gate, linking with Helmsley, Stokesley and Guisborough; occasional Moorsbus services run between Chop Gate, Carlton Bank and Osmotherley

Cringle Moor is undoubtedly one of the finest of the Cleveland Hills, its steep northern slopes looking northwards across the plains, while neighbouring hills rise close on either side. Walkers usually climb it from the Lord Stones Café on Carlton Bank in mere minutes, but the route offered here is a fine day's walk from Chop Gate (pronounced Chop 'Yat') in Bilsdale. The crest of Cold Moor is followed, then after crossing a gap, Cringle Moor is climbed using a steep and stony path. After enjoying fine views the route descends to the Lord Stones Café for a break, then traverses the moorlands on the western side of Bilsdale. Barker's Ridge leads to Noon Hill then a direct descent leads to Chop Gate.

Leave the car park at **Chop Gate** and follow the road up through the little village, passing the **Buck Inn**. Turn left at a road junction, then almost immediately right up a short cobbled road to a **Methodist church**. Go straight up a narrow, muddy, enclosed and often overgrown path. This becomes a fine grassy track later, and you go

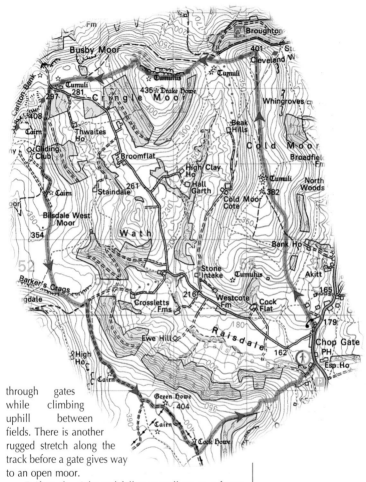

through gates while climbing uphill between fields. There is another rugged stretch along the track before a gate gives way to an open moor.

Drift to the right and follow a wall up to a forest, then drift to the left up a moorland path that can be rugged in places. Join and follow a clear track along the crest of the moorland, passing the heather humps of **Three Howes**. Cross a dip, then follow a clear but

87

Looking along the path from Cringle Moor to Lord Stones and Carlton Bank

narrow path past a cairn on the crest. Keep to the crest to reach the summit of **Cold Moor** at 401m (1316ft). The Cleveland Way is joined at this point, and you turn left to follow a stone-paved path straight downhill to a gap. Go through a gate as marked and reach an area of shale spoil. The path leading uphill is steep and stony, equipped with lots of little zigzags to ease the gradient a little. Eventually the slope begins to level out and a fine path curves round the abrupt northern edge of **Cringle Moor** around 420m (1380ft).

Follow the stone-paved or firm gritty path around the edge, then descend a little to reach a stone view-point seat dedicated to local rambler Alec Falconer at **Cringle End**. Turn left to continue the descent, using a stone-paved path running close to a drystone wall. Go through a gate at the bottom and walk along a grassy track flanked by a wall and a fence. Continue across a grassy common, but note that there is immediate access to **Lord Stones Café** and toilets in a car park surrounded by trees. The café is not too apparent as it is largely buried underground!

Cross a minor road and follow the stone-paved Cleveland Way up a bracken slope on **Carlton Bank**, but turn left and leave it to follow a track through a gate. Continue uphill until the track makes a pronounced bend to the right, at which point you leave it using a narrow path on the left, signposted as a bridleway. The path forges through heather to reach a track. Turn left along the track, which is broad and clear as it meanders around the moorland crest. Skirt round a rocky rash and later descend to the rushy pool of **Brian's Pond**.

Keep straight ahead, as signposted along a footpath, up what seems to be the clearest track from a junction of tracks, but which soon narrows to a path. It swings to the right of the moorland crest and enjoys views down into **Scugdale**. Pass to the right of a crag, then cross a stile and head back onto the heathery moorland crest as marked. There is a junction of paths and tracks, but you simply walk straight ahead to climb gently up the clearest track in view, going through a gate to continue up **Barker's Ridge**.

The broad, stony track is roughly aligned to the moorland crest, and the towering form of the Bilsdale transmitter is in view ahead. Looking back, note how the shapely form of Roseberry Topping seems to sail past the gap between Cringle Moor and Cold Moor. Turn left at a track junction and rise gently uphill. Look out for a stone upright pierced by a hole on **Green Howe** at 404m (1325ft). Keep to the track, but turn left later to reach another stone upright and cairn on **Cock Howe**.

Follow a narrow path onwards down a heather slope into Bilsdale. This is clear enough, and is augmented by blobs of paint, but is quite rugged in parts. Walk down the heather moor, then go straight down a steep and slippery slope of crumbling shale covered in bracken. Avoid a grooved path bending to the right. Cross a step-stile and continue down the path through fields. Cross stiles as required, then finally cross a wooden bridge over **Raisdale Beck** to return to the car park and toilets at **Chop Gate**.

Sunlight and shadow seen across
the head of Bilsdale from the higher moors

WALK 17
Chop Gate, Urra Moor, Hasty Bank and Cold Moor

Distance	15km (9.5 miles)
Start/finish	Chop Gate car park, Bilsdale, GR 558993
Maps	OS Landrangers 93 and 100; OS Explorer OL26 South and North Terrain A tough walk along firm, clear paths and tracks, though these can be muddy for short stretches; the high moors are exposed in bad weather
Refreshments	Buck Inn at Chop Gate, possibly a snack van on Clay Bank
Transport	Regular Moorsbus services run to Chop Gate and over Clay Bank, linking with Helmsley, Stokesley and Guisborough

The hills grouped around the head of Bilsdale offer a fine day's walk, and the tiny village of Chop Gate is a good starting point. A clear path and track offer an easy approach to Urra Moor, where Round Hill is the highest point in the North York Moors National Park. The course of the Cleveland Way can be followed down to a road on Clay Bank from where a steep climb leads onto the level top of Hasty Bank. The aggressive, chunky blocks known as the Wain Stones stand in complete contrast to the gently rolling moors. A walk along the crest of Cold Moor leads back into Bilsdale.

Leave the car park at **Chop Gate** and follow the road up through the little village, passing the **Buck Inn**. Follow the Stokesley road up and downhill, then turn right as signposted for St Hilda's Church. The road bends left at a higher level, near **Bilsdale Hall**, so turn right through a gate as indicated by a public bridleway signpost. A track drops a little in a wood, then climbs up from the wood. Note that you climb straight ahead and uphill from a gate, not along a track climbing to the right. Pass a shale spoil heap on a slope of bracken, then keep climbing to

91

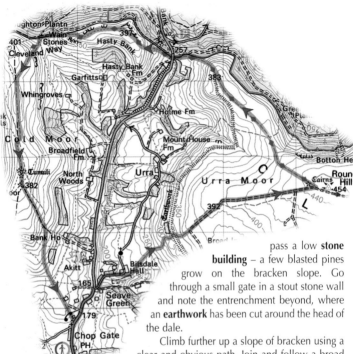

pass a low **stone building** – a few blasted pines grow on the bracken slope. Go through a small gate in a stout stone wall and note the entrenchment beyond, where an **earthwork** has been cut around the head of the dale.

Climb further up a slope of bracken using a clear and obvious path. Join and follow a broad and clear track that runs straight ahead, rising gently across heathery **Urra Moor**. Pass a few grouse-shooting butts, then later reach a junction of tracks. The idea is to turn left here, but you might want to follow a short narrow path to the trig point on top of **Round Hill**, at 454m (1490ft). This is the highest point in the North York Moors National Park, and while views may not be particularly dramatic, they are certainly extensive.

After turning left along the moorland track the course of the Cleveland Way is followed around the head of Bilsdale. A gritty or stone-paved path descends on a wide heather moorland slope. Cross a broad dip and eventually reach a gate on **Carr Ridge**. A stone-paved path drops steeply downhill. Go through a couple more small

ROUND HILL

The trig point on Round Hill sits on the squat remains of a moorland burial mound. The North York Moors are dotted with similar mounds, and some parts are crisscrossed by ancient earthworks that were either territorial markers or defensive structures. The moorland marker known as the Hand Stone probably dates from the 18th century. It has two open palms inscribed with the near-indecipherable words: 'this is the way to Stoxla [Stokesley]' and 'this is the way to Kirbie [Kirkbymoorside]'. The older Face Stone features a crudely carved face.

gates and reach the B1257 on **Clay Bank**. Regular Moorsbus services use this road, and while there *may* be a snack van parked away to the right, don't rely on it being there.

Cross the road and climb up the stone steps as signposted for the Cleveland Way. Cross a stile on the left and climb up a steep, stone-paved path on a bracken slope. This suddenly levels out as a stone-paved path along the moorland crest of **Hasty Bank**, around 390m (1280ft). Enjoy views stretching across the plains, as well as around Bilsdale. Keep to the right of the blocky outcrop of the **Wain Stones** to find a steep and rugged path downhill to a grassy gap. Climb from the gap and go through a gate, then turn left to leave the Cleveland Way and take a path climbing diagonally uphill.

Turn left along a moorland crest and follow a narrow but clear path past a cairn around 390m (1280ft) on **Cold Moor**. Keep going across a slight dip on the heathery crest and continue along a clear track. Pass the heather humps of **Three Howes** and fork left along a rugged path to

The jagged gritstone outcrops of the Wain Stones seen on Hasty Bank

A gateway is passed above a grassy gap between Hasty Bank and Cold Moor

start descending a moorland slope. This path approaches a forest, then follows a wall down to a gate. Go through the gate to find a rugged enclosed track that can be muddy. Go through gates on the way downhill between fields, and at first the track becomes easy and grassy, though later it narrows and becomes muddy and over-grown. It suddenly pops out beside a **Methodist church**, and a short cobbled road leads down to a tarmac road. Turn left then almost immediately right to follow the B1257 down through **Chop Gate**. Pass the Buck Inn on the way back to the car park and toilets where you started.

WALK 18
Kildale, Ingleby Moor and Battersby Moor

Distance	17km (10.5 miles) if starting from Kildale Railway Station, or 11km (6.25 miles) if using a car to start from the road on Warren Moor
Start/finish	Kildale Railway Station, GR 604095
Maps	OS Landranger 94; OS Explorer OL26 North
Terrain	A fairly easy walk along minor roads and moorland tracks, with one less-trodden path, but the high moors are exposed in bad weather
Refreshments	Two tea rooms at Kildale
Transport	Arriva trains run to Kildale from Whitby and Middlesbrough

Kildale is a tiny village with good access to the Cleveland Hills. This route follows a road from Kildale onto Warren Moor, then takes a path down to Baysdale Abbey. Good tracks are used to climb onto Ingleby Moor, then the course of the Cleveland Way is followed over Battersby Moor to return to Warren Moor. The walk is structured from the railway station at Kildale, but cars can be driven up the road to Warren Moor and parked, which shortens the walk by 6km (3.75 miles). Alternatively, this walk can be combined with Walk 19, also starting from Kildale, to offer a much longer day's exploration.

Leave **Kildale Railway Station**, where there are toilets, and walk up the road, passing Glebe Cottage tea room. Turn right to pass **Kildale Village Store**, which is a post office shop also offering teas. Leave the little village and turn left along another road at a junction, heading straight towards the steep slopes of **Park Nab**. The road heads off to the right and climbs uphill, swinging right until it crosses a cattle-grid on a high corner of the road on **Warren Moor**, at 335m (1099ft). (Motorists could park

95

beside this high road, which will be followed again later in the day.)

A public bridleway signpost points left to indicate a narrow path across the heather moor. Walk downhill, roughly parallel to a line of old fenceposts and a drystone wall. Go through a small gate and look downhill through a rough pasture to spot another small gate. Go through it and walk further downhill, turning right to reach a narrow tarmac road. Turn left down the road and cross a bridge to approach the big house of **Baysdale Abbey**, which has several farm buildings alongside. The house stands on the site of a 12th-century Cistercian nunnery, of which little remains.

Turn right before reaching the house and farmyard, and go through a gate bearing a waymark arrow to enter a large field. Veer slightly left across the field to spot a gate at a point where a wall and fence meet. Go through the gate and climb up through the next field to reach another gate giving access to a **forest**. Fork right along a track immediately on entering the forest. The track can be rather wet and slimy as it winds uphill, but it becomes a lovely grassy carpet before it leaves the forest at yet another gate.

Continue along and up the grassy track on a moorland crest of heather and bilberry, with the track becoming stony as it passes the stump of

96

The Guide Stone is a moorland marker where cash is left for needy travellers!

an old **stone cross** set in a socket. Further uphill, on the right, is a gritstone outcrop. The track rises further and eventually levels out on **Ingleby Moor**. Avoid a track heading off to the right, but wait until the track you are following runs slightly downhill, then take the next clear stony track to the right. This track bends to the left as it climbs, then runs straight up the heathery slope with boundary stones alongside. It reaches the ancient tumulus of **Burton Howe** at 424m (1391ft) and joins another clear track.

Turn right to follow the track downhill alongside **Greenhow Bank**. This is part of the Cleveland Way, which is followed all the way back to Kildale, but first keep an eye peeled to spot the **Guide Stone** away to the right.

GUIDE STONE

From 1711 it was a requirement that signposts and guidestones were erected on remote moorland routes, and the stone markers outlived wooden ones. The 18th-century Guide Stone is easily missed in poor visibility, lying well away from the track. It offers the following directions: 'Ingleby and Stoxley [Stokesley]', 'Kirby [Kirkbymoorside] and Helmsley', and 'Gisbro [Guisborough]'. Of interest to cash-strapped walkers is a hollow on top of the stone that usually contains a few coins left for needy wayfarers.

Keep walking northwards along the track until another track, signposted for the Cleveland Way, branches off to the right at a gate. This track leads along another moorland crest over **Battersby Moor**, eventually reaching a gate at a road bend. Follow the road straight ahead. (Motorists who parked here earlier in the day finish at this point.) The road crosses a rise on **Warren Moor**, turns left over a cattle-grid at a corner, then runs down around the slopes of **Park Nab** to reach a broad and green valley. When a road junction is reached, turn right for **Kildale**. To return to the railway station, turn left as signposted.

WALK 19
Kildale, Leven Vale, Baysdale and Hograh Moor

Distance	16km (10 miles)
Start/finish	Kildale Railway Station, GR 604095
Maps	OS Landranger 94; OS Explorer OL26 North
Terrain	A moderate walk along clear tracks and paths, though some parts are more rugged; minor roads are used at the start and finish
Refreshments	Two tea rooms at Kildale
Transport	Arriva trains run to Kildale from Whitby and Middlesbrough

Just one obscure road leads to the farming settlement at the head of Baysdale, and another road crosses the barren moorland slopes in the middle of the dale. Only those who are prepared to stride along its moorland flanks can discover the old tracks and paths that once carried all the traffic in and out of the dale. This route, starting and finishing in Kildale, also includes little Leven Vale, where the remains of an old ironstone mine can be seen. At another point the route is only a short walk from the little village of Westerdale, though this is barely in view.

Leave **Kildale Railway Station**, where there are toilets, and walk up the road, passing Glebe Cottage tea room. Turn left as signposted for Commondale. Walk alongside the boundary wall encircling **Kildale Hall**, then turn right as signposted for **Little Kildale**. Pass the few cottages that make up this tiny settlement and follow the road up a forested slope. It becomes a broad dirt road as it climbs from the forest into fields. Turn right as signposted along a public bridleway just before reaching **Warren Farm**. Walk down through a field, noting a **chimney** that is the only remaining part of the former Warren Moor Ironstone Mine in **Leven Vale**.

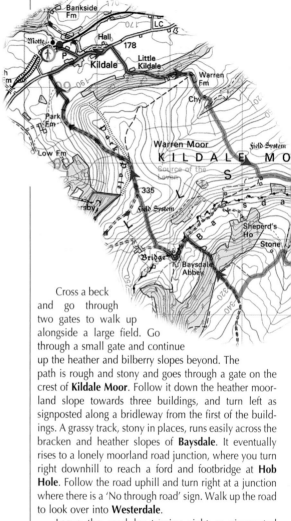

Cross a beck and go through two gates to walk up alongside a large field. Go through a small gate and continue up the heather and bilberry slopes beyond. The path is rough and stony and goes through a gate on the crest of **Kildale Moor**. Follow it down the heather moorland slope towards three buildings, and turn left as signposted along a bridleway from the first of the buildings. A grassy track, stony in places, runs easily across the bracken and heather slopes of **Baysdale**. It eventually rises to a lonely moorland road junction, where you turn right downhill to reach a ford and footbridge at **Hob Hole**. Follow the road uphill and turn right at a junction where there is a 'No through road' sign. Walk up the road to look over into **Westerdale**.

Leave the road by turning right as signposted along a public bridleway and follow a cart-rut track up the heather slopes of **Little Hograh Moor**. This soon becomes a rutted path across the slope, marked with cairns, crossing a small beck. Later, **Great Hograh Moor** is quite bouldery and the path passes a memorial cairn. Walk down to cross a neat little arched stone bridge next to a gnarled oak tree in **Great Hograh Beck**. Climb straight uphill and turn left up a clear track. Follow this up a heather moorland slope and continue until a junction is reached with another clear track. Turn right here and walk downhill, eventually going through a gate into a **forest**. Keep to the clearest track and emerge at a house.

Go down the access track away from the house and turn left to walk alongside **Baysdale Beck**. Turn right to walk through a farmyard and pass close to the big house of **Baysdale Abbey**. The house stands on the site of a 12th-century Cistercian nunnery, of which little remains. Follow the tarmac access road across a bridge and head uphill a short way. Turn right at a bridleway signpost, then turn left to walk uphill and go through a small gate. Look up a slope of rough pasture to spot another small gate, then walk uphill and go through it. A heather moorland is reached and a narrow path runs parallel to a wall and a line of old fenceposts. It reaches 335m (1099ft) on **Warren Moor**, where there is a road and a cattle-grid.

Turn right to cross the cattle-grid and follow the road down around the slopes of **Park Nab** to reach a broad and green valley. When a road junction is reached, turn right for **Kildale**, passing the village store, which is a post office shop also offering teas. To return to the **railway station** and toilets, turn left as signposted.

Walkers forge their way across the heather slopes of Little Hograh Moor

THE NORTHERN MOORS

The Northern Moors rear up from the plains with great gusto, Roseberry Topping – the Yorkshire Matterhorn – in particular raising rugged flanks to a fine peak. There are other steep slopes nearby, such as those rising to Easby Moor and Captain Cook's Monument, or the forested slopes rising from Guisborough, but on the whole the Northern Moors lack distinctive features, and present a vista of gently rolling uplands of no great height, petering out eastwards as cultivated fields and wooded valleys lead to the coast.

Wild moorland walking is quite limited in this area. Walkers who have followed the course of the Cleveland Way will recall the prominent monument on Easby Moor, and the arduous detour out to Roseberry Topping. They will also recall the fiddly nature of the route through Guisborough Woods, and the way the route seems to forsake the high ground altogether, leaving the national park and heading across country to reach the coast at Saltburn. It takes a bit more effort to discover the Northern Moors, as well as careful route-finding where paths are not particularly well trodden. The area used to be crisscrossed with prominent tracks, but the moorland has almost engulfed them, leaving only rugged grooves and occasional lengths of stone-flagged causeways.

Four walking routes are described in this area. The first is a popular circuit from Great Ayton, taking in Easby Moor and Roseberry Topping. Next is a walk from Guisborough, wandering over Gisborough Moor. A route from Danby takes in the empty moorlands around Siss Cross, but also links some of the villages along the flanks of Eskdale. A final route runs from Scalby Dam to Danby, offering the chance to visit the Moors Centre before heading back over Danby Beacon. Paths can be quite vague, but the discovery of travellers' ancient trails is one of the delights of walking over these moors.

Public transport around the Northern Moors is remarkably good, and the area can be approached on a daily basis throughout the year using Arriva buses and trains that run from early until late. Additional Moorsbus services run to and from the Moors Centre near Danby, where visitors to the North York Moors National Park can obtain plenty of information about the area.

WALK 20
Great Ayton, Easby Moor and Roseberry Topping

Distance	11km (6.5 miles)
Start/finish	High Green, Great Ayton, GR 563107
Maps	OS Landranger 93; OS Explorer OL26 North
Terrain	A short walk, but tough in places, along clear roads, tracks and paths, with some steep slopes
Refreshments	Royal Oak Hotel at Great Ayton
Transport	Regular Arriva buses serve Great Ayton from Stokesley and Guisborough, Arriva rail goes to Great Ayton from Middlesbrough and Whitby, and there are regular Moorsbus services to Great Ayton from Guisborough and Helmsley

Walkers regularly visit Captain Cook's Monument on Easby Moor and climb the 'Yorkshire Matterhorn' of Roseberry Topping. This route starts in the village of Great Ayton, where James Cook was educated, and heads along an old incline railway before climbing onto Ayton Moor. After inspecting the monument the route follows the course of the Cleveland Way to stay high and reach Roseberry Topping. After enjoying views from the summit walkers can descend to Aireyholme Farm, where James Cook lived as a youth, and ponder whether he ever climbed Roseberry Topping! Various paths are linked to return through the fields to Great Ayton.

Start on the High Green in the village of **Great Ayton**. There is a pub here, a few shops, even a bank and a post office, as well as toilets and a tourist information centre, ☎ 01684 722835. Follow **Station Road** and later cross the bridge over the line at **Great Ayton Railway Station**, then turn right along a short access road signposted as a public footpath. Go through a gate at the end of the track and cross a beck. Go over a stile beside a gate and turn right along a track to go through a nearby gate. Turn left along another track, which is actually an old railway trackbed running parallel to the current railway line. It passes a brick-built tower. When a broad turning space is reached, bear left up an old **incline railway** trackbed, passing an old reservoir. Note the reddish spoil heaps

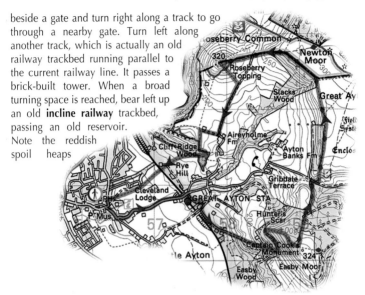

from old ironstone mines further uphill. There are views of Roseberry Topping and the Cleveland Hills rising from the plains. At the top of the incline the stone foundations of the old winding house can be inspected.

Climb a little further to reach a gateway and a blue marker arrow. Don't go through the gate, but turn left along a path and go through another gate later. Before the path starts dropping any more steeply downhill, turn right up to a gateway in a wall at the corner of a **forest**. Climb straight up a clear, worn path, cross a grassy track and continue straight up through the forest. A grassy path leads out onto the heather top of **Easby Moor**, and you will naturally be drawn straight to the prominent stone obelisk of **Captain Cook's Monument**, standing at 324m (1063ft).

Turn left to follow a stone-paved path away from the monument and walk down a track on a forested slope. Turn right along a minor road at **Gribdale Gate**, then almost immediately left up a flight of steps on a slope of

CAPTAIN COOK'S MONUMENT

This fine stone obelisk is 15m (51ft) high and overlooks Marton, the suburb of Middlesbrough where James Cook was born in 1728, and Great Ayton, where he received an education from 1736 to 1740. Cook's father was employed at Aireyholme Farm, where Mr Scottowe paid for James' education at the Michael Postgate School, now the Captain Cook Schoolroom Museum. The inscription on the obelisk states, 'In memory of Captain Cook the celebrated navigator. A man in nautical knowledge inferior to none. In zeal, prudence and energy superior to most. Regardless of the danger he opened an intercourse with the Friendly Isles and other parts of the Southern Hemisphere. Born at Marton in 1728. Massacred at Owhyee [Hawaii] 1779.'

The prominent little peak of Roseberry Topping is seen here at sunset

bracken. The gradient eases on **Great Ayton Moor**, where there is a wall and forest to the left and heather moorland to the right. Simply follow a clear track onwards, around 290m (950ft), with the wall always to the left. The wall suddenly turns a corner on **Newton Moor** where there is a gate and a signpost for Roseberry Topping. Zigzag down a stone-paved path and cross a grassy gap, then zigzag up a stone-paved path, passing a commemorative stone for the Cleveland Way (distances are given as Helmsley 46 miles and Filey 64 miles). Slabs

of sandstone and a trig point mark the summit of **Roseberry Topping** at 320m (1050ft).

ROSEBERRY TOPPING

Quarried and scarred, undermined for ironstone, leading to partial collapse in 1907, Roseberry Topping has suffered greatly through the years, but has by no means been diminished. The Yorkshire Matterhorn bears its scars proudly and presents an aggressive face to the plains. Enjoy the views from this airy perch, looking out across the plains to the distant Pennines and industrial Teesmouth, as well as round the Cleveland Hills and North York Moors, even taking in a small stretch of the Cleveland coast.

Retrace your steps back across slabs of rock, but fork right down another stone-paved path to descend a steep slope of bracken. Go through a small gate and walk down a grassy slope to pass through a large gate at the bottom. Turn right down a clear track, going through a gate to approach **Aireyholme Farm**. Walk through a gate and almost into the farmyard, but turn right through another gate signposted as a public footpath. Follow a track up alongside a field to a little **cottage**, and turn left alongside a fence as marked. (You could make a detour onto the rugged little hill where hard 'whinstone' was quarried until 1973, though the area is now the Cliff Rigg Quarry Nature Reserve.)

Follow the fence to a corner and turn left to cross a step-stile, then cross another stile nearby to walk down a path on a wooded slope. Continue straight through a junction of paths to enter a field, then swing right. From that point always walk straight ahead through the fields, crossing an access road, then crossing a **railway line** with care. Again, take care when the path eventually emerges on an awkward bend on **Newton Road**. Turn left to walk back to the finish point at the High Green in Great Ayton.

WALK 21
Guisborough, Gisborough Moor and Hutton Village

Distance	15km (9.5 miles)
Start/finish	Market place, Guisborough, GR 615160
Maps	OS Landrangers 93 and 94; OS Explorer OL26 North
Terrain	A moderate walk along good forest and moorland paths and tracks, but some paths are virtually untrodden; a low-level railway trackbed is used at the end
Refreshments	Plenty of pubs, restaurants and cafés around Guisborough
Transport	Regular Arriva buses serve Guisborough from places including Whitby, Stokesley and Middlesbrough

Guisborough is a bustling little town with a broad main street flanked by cobbled areas. Its most outstanding feature is a ruined priory set in a quiet green space near the town centre. Extensive woods and forest fill the slope between the town and Gisborough Moor, and the Cleveland Way traverses that slope. Paths and tracks over the moor can be confusing, but it is worth the effort to explore such a quiet corner of the North York Moors. The return route uses a very clear moorland track, as well as following the course of a disused railway line through the suburbs from Hutton Village to Guisborough.

Start in the market place in **Guisborough**, and maybe take the time to visit the priory ruins, or save a visit until later. Follow **Bow Street**, which is the way the traffic goes to Whitby, but when most vehicles turn left, keep straight on along **Belmangate**. At the top end of the road is a care home where a public footpath sign points further uphill. The path is flanked by hedgerows as it climbs between fields to reach the lower edge of **Guisborough Woods**.

Climb straight uphill and cross a forest track. Climb straight uphill again along a track that can be muddy. When this track bends left, branch right instead and climb further uphill to reach another forest track (used by the Cleveland Way). Turn left to follow it uphill again until it levels out, with views back to Guisborough and further afield to industrial Teesmouth. Turn right at a junction and follow another track, crossing one final track before a small gate gives way to the open slopes of **Gisborough Moor**.

Follow a clear path straight ahead and gently up the heather moorland slope. Watch out for a cairn well to the right later, and head across pathless moorland to reach it – it stands over 320m (1050ft). Turn left along a grassy and quite obvious track nearby and follow it onwards. However, the public footpath that heads down to the right towards Sleddale is practically untrodden on the ground. Some walkers may prefer to stay on the track, and later make a pronounced right turn at a junction to follow another track downhill. This leads to the remote farmstead at **Sleddale**. Go through a gate and pass the farm to follow its access road.

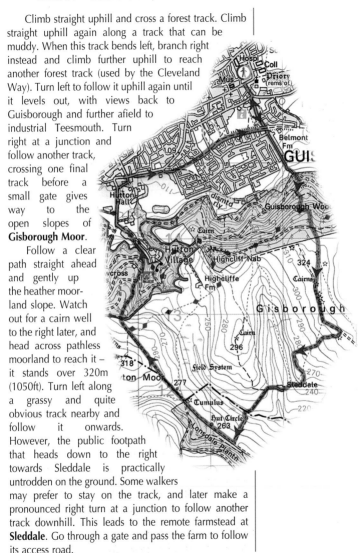

The farm access road crosses another little valley on its way up to a road junction on **Percy Cross Rigg**. Turn right and walk up the road at a gentle gradient, passing an enclosure containing five Iron Age hut circles. The tarmac road ends at a gate and a sandy track rises beyond, signposted as a public bridleway, and becoming rough and stony as it gains height. Pass a wartime pillbox at the top, around 300m (985ft), then head downhill. Note the course of the Cleveland Way to the right before reaching a forest gate.

Go through the gate and follow the track straight downhill through **Hutton Lowcross Woods**, avoiding all other tracks on the slope to land on a road just outside **Hutton village**. Follow Hutton village road through a sort of grassy parkland where fine individual trees spread their boughs. Watch out for the access roads for **Hutton Hall** and the White House, both of which are private, but just alongside is a short access road signposted as a public footpath. Follow this and it narrows to become a path leading to a junction with busy **Hutton Lane**.

Follow the lane a little way towards town to find nearby bus stops, as well as a step-stile giving access to

A fine track is followed for a while over the higher parts of Gisborough Moor

an old wooded railway trackbed running parallel to the road. Follow the trackbed from an old station platform and later walk along a bit of **Aldenham Road** to pick up another stretch of the old line alongside a row of houses. The line runs through a green space between modern housing estates, then you cross a road and find two old trackbeds branching apart – keep right to follow a trackbed on a wooded embankment. It leads to a bridge over **Belmangate**, but you should go down steps on the left just before the bridge. A left turn leads straight back into **Guisborough**.

A cyclist on the old moorland track between Percy Cross Rigg and Hutton village

GISBOROUGH PRIORY

Founded in 1119 by Robert de Brus, Gisborough Priory was a powerful Augustinian house. The priory church was rebuilt around 1200, but was destroyed in 1289 by a fire caused by a plumber working on the roof. Many artefacts were also lost in the blaze. After rebuilding, the priory was again wrecked by raiding Scots, but eventually it assumed its full stature, which visitors can still appreciate to some extent by marvelling at the towering arch of the east window. There is an entrance charge, and the priory also incorporates a tourist information centre, ☎ 01287 633801.

WALK 22
Danby, Siss Cross, Commondale and Castleton

Distance	14km (8.75 miles)
Start/finish	Danby Railway Station, GR 707084
Maps	OS Landranger 94; OS Explorer OL26 North
Terrain	A moderate moorland walk where the initial moorland path needs careful route-finding, but other paths and tracks are clear, ending with a low-level valley walk
Refreshments	Duke of Wellington and a café at Danby, Cleveland Inn and a tea shop at Commondale, Eskdale Inn off-route at Castleton
Transport	Regular Moorsbus services to Danby from Pickering, Helmsley and Guisborough; Arriva trains from Whitby and Middlesbrough link Commondale, Castleton and Danby

The little village of Danby in Eskdale is a natural starting point for walks, having regular Moorsbus and rail services. This day's walk climbs onto Danby Low Moor and visits Siss Cross before heading down to Commondale. A low-level walk along tracks leads from Commondale towards Castleton and so back through the dale to Danby. Of course the walk could be finished early, or altered in terms of start and finish, by catching a train at any of the three railway stations – Danby, Commondale and Castleton. With more time to spare, walkers could head for Danby Lodge and the Moors Centre, though a visit here is also included in Walk 23.

Leave the railway station and walk straight up the road through the village of **Danby**, passing the Duke of Wellington pub. There is also a shop and café nearby. The road uphill is signposted for Scaling and Whitby, and crosses a cattle-grid. Continue up a bendy stretch of the road at **Rosedale Intake** to reach a moorland slope where the road runs straight ahead. A sign reading 'Danby' is mounted

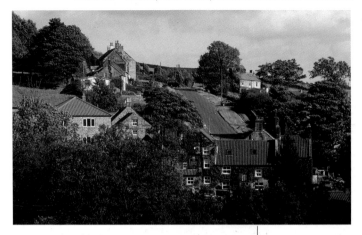

on a roadside stone, and you turn left as indicated by a public footpath signpost. Be sure not to follow the broad grassy path, but keep a little to the right along a narrower trodden path. This path forges up the gentle heather slopes of **Danby Low Moor** and crosses a path known as the Pannierman's Causeway. The way uphill is occasionally marked with yellow blobs of paint or small cairns. For reference, it heads for an upright stone that can be seen on the skyline, and this is **Siss Cross**, standing at 268m (879ft). Enjoy sweeping views across Eskdale to the High Moors.

The little Eskdale village of Danby has good Moorsbus and railway connections

The stone upright of Siss Cross offers views around the bleak moorlands

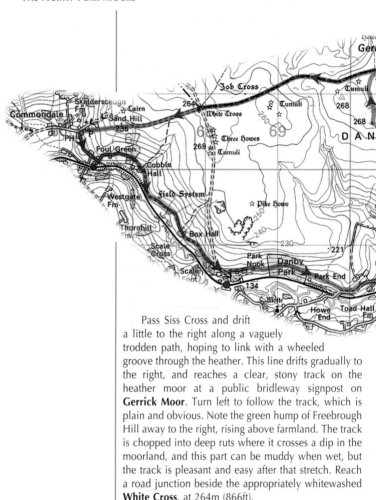

Pass Siss Cross and drift
a little to the right along a vaguely
trodden path, hoping to link with a wheeled
groove through the heather. This line drifts gradually to
the right, and reaches a clear, stony track on the
heather moor at a public bridleway signpost on
Gerrick Moor. Turn left to follow the track, which is
plain and obvious. Note the green hump of Freebrough
Hill away to the right, rising above farmland. The track
is chopped into deep ruts where it crosses a dip in the
moorland, and this part can be muddy when wet, but
the track is pleasant and easy after that stretch. Reach
a road junction beside the appropriately whitewashed
White Cross, at 264m (866ft).

Walk straight ahead along and down the road signposted for Commondale, which is much quieter than
the other road on the moorland slope. Before the road
rises on **Sand Hill** watch out for a public bridleway

signpost on the left. Pick up stretches of a flagged causeway across a slope of bracken, then later turn left and go down through three small gates to reach the little village of **Commondale**. Notice the preponderance of brick buildings, rather than stone, as the village was essentially founded on a brickworks. The Cleveland Inn offers food and drink, and there is a tea shop, as well as toilets.

Turn left along a minor road as signposted for the station. Fork left at **Foul Green farm**, and the station can be found down to the right if required. However, to continue with the route stay on the track and climb uphill for a while to enjoy good views over Eskdale. The track runs through oak and birch woods before dropping down to a few houses at **Cobble Hall**. Follow the track across a moorland slope above, and roughly parallel to, the railway line. The track passes **Box Hall** and rises to cross a cattle-grid at **Firbank** where a minor road is reached. Turn right downhill, passing a sign for **Castleton** mounted on a roadside stone. This road could be followed all the way down to the railway station or the Eskdale Inn, but the route doesn't go that far, turning instead left along a farm access track signposted as a bridleway.

Pass farm buildings at **Park Nook**, and go through a couple of gates to follow a grassy track gently down to a gate leading into woods at **Danby Park**. The woodland is mostly birch and a clear path runs across the slope to exit at another gate. Follow a grassy path straight onwards across a bracken slope, and continue straight ahead along and down a minor road. There are two public footpath signposts on the right later – one in a dip and one over the next rise on the road. Either of them could be used to return directly to Danby Railway Station, but many walkers might prefer to continue along the road to reach the Duke of Wellington and have a break before leaving.

WALK 23
Scaling Dam, Clitherbeck, Danby and Becon Hill

Distance	14km (8.75 miles)
Start/finish	Scaling Reservoir Water Sports, GR 740125
Maps	OS Landranger 94; OS Explorer OL27 North
Terrain	A moderate moorland walk where vague or untrodden paths at the start and finish need care; other moorland paths, tracks and roads are clear
Refreshments	Grapes Inn at Scaling Dam, Duke of Wellington and a café at Danby, café at the Moors Centre
Transport	Regular Arriva buses pass Scaling Dam, regular Moorsbus services to Danby from Pickering, Helmsley and Guisborough, and Arriva trains serve Danby from Whitby and Middlesbrough

Traffic hurtles along the busy A171 at Scaling Dam and there is also a good bus service along the road. From here some remarkably bleak moorlands can be discovered using all-but-forgotten paths and tracks. One such path is the Pannierman's Causeway, which is virtually lost in its early stages, but gradually reveals its course and ultimately becomes a fine flagstone causeway. Lord's Turnpike is a good track leading down to Danby, and offers a chance to visit the Moors Centre. Danby Beacon makes a fine viewpoint, taking in the Northern Moors and High Moors, before a track across the moors gradually fades on the way back to Scaling Dam.

There is a car park at Scaling Reservoir Water Sports, not far from the Grapes Inn at **Scaling Dam**, safely off the busy main A171. Apart from the sailing club premises there are toilets and bird hides, and the western end of the reservoir is a nature reserve to which there is no public access. Start the walk by leaving the car park and turning left to walk along busy **Moor Road**. Walk on the right-hand side, on the grass verge, facing oncoming traffic for safety. Continue to the road junction signposted for Grinkle and walk just a short distance beyond it on **Waupley Moor**.

There is a public bridleway signpost and a small gate on the left-hand side of the main road. Go through the gate and swing to the right among some gorse bushes to find a vaguely trodden path. This leads to a **gravel strip** across a boggy patch then the trodden route expires. Pass a nearby **tree** and aim southwest towards a vague dip in the skyline ahead, pushing through a large patch of bracken to reach heather moorland beyond. Look carefully for a groove in the heather which leads to a prominent upright **boundary stone** with two smaller stones crouched beside it. However, step to the right to reach a smaller upright stone nearby.

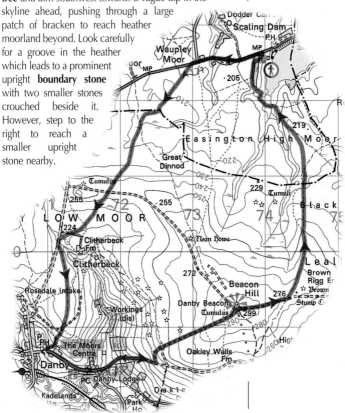

The old flagstone surface of the
Pannierman's Causeway crosses the moors

Follow a vaguely trodden path onwards through the heather to approach a large rushy area in a dip, and be sure to spot a **wooden post** that marks the position of a low **footbridge** offering the only dry-footed passage through a bog. Once across, follow a narrow trodden path that weaves gradually uphill through a series of parallel grooves on a heather moorland slope. Pass a few gorse bushes and a small lonesome pine tree, and note a **marker stone** where old grooved pathways intersect. The placenames on it are almost indecipherable, though 'Whitby' is written as 'BY WHIT' on one face, and 'Castleton' may be vaguely discerned on another face.

Step across a minor road as signposted public bridleway, at almost 250m (820ft), then continue down a groove in the heather moorland. Watch carefully to spot a flagged causeway, and follow it – this is the **Pannierman's Causeway**, and it is good to see at least some stretches of it running clearly across the moor. Step across a farm access track near **Clitherbeck** and aim for a road crossing a stream nearby. Once the road has crossed the stream turn left along a clear track signposted as a public bridleway. This is obvious underfoot all the way across a heather moor. When a drystone wall is reached, swing right at a complex junction of tracks and be sure to take the track that drops most steeply down towards the village of Danby. Go through a gate and, near some houses, reach a battered road that quickly leads onto another road. Either turn right down Briar Hill to go into the village of **Danby**, or left along Lodge Lane to reach the Moors Centre at **Danby Lodge**, where this route heads.

THE MOORS CENTRE

Danby Lodge used to be a shooting lodge but now serves as a visitor centre for the North York Moors National Park. Displays and exhibits focus on conservation, in order to encourage sensitive and thoughtful recreation. Maps and guides are on sale, and there is a café and toilets on site. The countryside nearby is open for exploration and regular Moorsbus services run from the centre, to encourage visitors to leave their cars behind. To check opening times, ☎ 01287 660654.

Leave the **Moors Centre** and take the road sign-posted for Danby Beacon, following it uphill through fields and over a cattle-grid. Turn left at a road junction and the road bends right before running straight up to the highest part of the heather moorland. The summit of **Danby Beacon** is cluttered with a signpost, tumulus, view indicator and a trig point at 299m (981ft). Views around the northern half of the North York Moors are particularly extensive.

Walk gently downhill along a broad and stony track signposted for Lealholm. Turn left as signposted along a public bridleway, and immediately fork right along a grassy path that soon narrows on heathery **Lealholm Moor**. Although narrow, the path has a few cairns along its length and is clear enough to follow easily. An area of short-cropped grass is reached, next to a little valley where there are a few trees, on **Easington High Moor**. A track slices off to the right, broad and clear, and the right of way is supposed to branch left from it later, but is quite invisible on the moorland. It is better not to follow the track, but to proceed along the moorland brow over-looking the valley, but do not enter the valley as it is difficult to negotiate. Head towards the reservoir, which can be seen ahead, and a fence will lead down to the left to reveal a gate and **footbridge**.

Cross the footbridge and walk along a duckboard path between fences. Head uphill to the left, and then turn right and go through a gate. A grassy track heads straight towards busy **Moor Road**, but before reaching it turn right along a footpath that leads through a small wood to return directly to the car park beside the reservoir.

THE HIGH MOORS

For many walkers the High Moors are the best part of the North York Moors National Park – extensive rolling moorlands are cleft by a dozen verdant dales, the plateau-like nature of the uplands being determined by the sandstone cap that protects lower, softer and more crumbly limestones and shales from weathering. The sandstone generates a rather acidic soil that favours moorland vegetation, and some wetter parts develop peat bogs. The limestones and shales exposed in the deeper dales allow grasslands suitable for pasture to flourish, and some of the level areas may even be tilled.

The High Moors are crisscrossed with paths and tracks. Many of the paths are based on ancient cross-country trading routes linking one dalehead with another, while other routes avoided the dales altogether and soared across broad moorland 'riggs' to get through the region as quickly as possible. Many of the ancient routes were waymarked by stone 'crosses'. In some cases these were actually carved as crosses, while in others they were simply squared stumps of rock inscribed with various place-names, and many of the old inscriptions are now barely decipherable. They were often carved by barely literate hands and contain wildly inaccurate and variable spellings! Later tracks were installed to allow vehicle access for grouse shooting and general moorland management.

A dozen fine walks explore the High Moors, and many of the routes lie close to each other or have a path in common, so there is scope to switch from one to another, varying and extending the routes. Two walks start from Chop Gate at the head of Bilsdale, exploring the moors on either side of the dale, and two more wander high above Farndale. Two walks explore Spaunton Moor, one from Hutton-le-Hole and the other from Rosedale, and two are based on the old Rosedale Railway, one making a circuit around the dale and the other running from Blakey to Battersby – from the moors to the plains. One walk explores Westerdale, while another three start from villages in Eskdale and climb high above Danby Dale, Great Fryup Dale and Glaisdale. Nor is that the end of the matter, since the course of the Lyke Wake Walk is covered towards the end of this guidebook. It stays as high as possible on the High Moors, enjoying some of the places already visited, and including additional tracts of broad, bleak and barren moorlands.

In the summer months, when the heather is in bloom and the High Moors are flushed purple, they are a joy to explore. But in foul weather, poor visibility, or when winter weather whips across them, they are best left to those who are good navigators. Even though many of the paths and tracks used are clear and well trodden, a wrong turning can lead well off-course and cause a lot of inconvenience late in the day.

WALK 24
Chop Gate, Cock Howe, Ryedale and Wetherhouse Moor

Distance	20km (12.5 miles), or 14.5km (9 miles) using the Moorsbus service back from Fangdale Beck
Start/finish	Chop Gate car park, Bilsdale, GR 558993
Maps	OS Landranger 100; OS Explorer OL26 South
Terrain	A tough walk, mostly along clear moorland paths and tracks, but some stretches are virtually untrodden; the high moors are exposed, but low-level field paths are used from farm to farm later in the day
Refreshments	Buck Inn at Chop Gate
Transport	Regular Moorsbus services pass Chop Gate and Fangdale Beck, linking with Helmsley, Stokesley and Guisborough; occasional Moorsbus services between Chop Gate and Osmotherley

This walk starts at Chop Gate (pronounced Chop 'Yat') at the head of Bilsdale and crosses from Bilsdale to Ryedale, then back to Bilsdale, exploring two parts of the broad and bleak expanse of Bilsdale West Moor. The immensely tall Bilsdale transmitter is like a pivot to the walk and remains a prominent feature in views throughout the day. After descending to the little village of Fangdale Beck the route wanders from farm to farm on the valley sides back to Chop Gate. The low-level stretch could be omitted if you land on the road in time to catch one of the Moorsbus services back to Chop Gate.

Leave the back of the car park at **Chop Gate** and cross a wooden bridge over Raisdale Beck. Follow a track up from a gate as marked, but watch for a footpath sign pointing up to the left. Climb straight uphill, crossing stiles as marked and avoiding a marker pointing left. There is a steep, crumbling, slippery shale path on a bracken slope. This path levels out on a heather moor,

and although fairly clear it can be rugged in places and is marked with paint blobs. There is a cairn and an upright stone on **Cock Howe** around 400m (1310ft).

Continue straight onwards, crossing a track, to follow a narrow but obvious path down a heather moor. This leads to a beck that is crossed beside a large, split, half-dead and half-living rowan tree. Climb uphill and keep to the right-hand side of a wall on a grassy moorland, later reaching the access track leading away from **Head House**. Turn right to follow the track gently uphill across the moorland slopes of **Arnsgill Ridge**, then there is a gradual descent. Go through a gate and down a track through fields to **Rye Farm**.

Turn left as marked by a yellow arrow on a gate *before* reaching the farm access track. Walk down a steep, rugged grassy slope and forge through a wet rushy patch to find a footbridge over **Arns Gill**. Climb up to a small gate in a wall and go through, then turn right up a deep-cut groove full of heather and bilberry. This can be a drag on the feet, but a stony and grassy track continues alongside a wall then leads down the moorland slope, through a gate and onto a minor road in **Ryedale**.

The tiny village of Chop Gate (pronounced Chop 'Yat') at the head of Bilsdale

123

Turn left to follow the road beside a wood, then later the road wriggles downhill to **Lane House Farm** where there is a public bridleway signpost pointing left through a gate. Walk down through a field and through another gate, then down through the next field and swing left through a gap. Walk down to a gate and ford **Blow Gill** in a wooded valley. Follow a narrow path up a bracken slope, away from the river onto a heather moor. Keep following the only narrow path uphill, and if you lose it, don't worry, but simply climb straight up and aim for the trees on the moorland crest ahead, which will reveal the semi-derelict farmstead of **Low Thwaites**.

Turn left to follow a clear track alongside a wall, heading gradually uphill. Turn right around a corner of the wall, then look for a narrow path heading off to the left, linking a line of posts planted across **Wetherhouse Moor**. The path and posts lead down into a shallow valley on the moorland where a little beck is crossed in a wet and boggy area. Continue along the narrow path, in a heathery groove, to pass a cairn on the moorland slope. Follow the path faithfully, as it is the only real trodden route downhill. Take care when following it more steeply down a deep groove on a bracken slope, as the ground underfoot is uneven. Go through a couple of small gates, down a field, through a gate and turn right. Turn left out of a garden at the Forge and walk along a tarmac road through the little village of **Fangdale Beck**.

Either walk to a telephone at a road junction and turn left along the B1257, or cross a **footbridge** over the River Seph, climb up steps, then turn left along the road. (If a Moorsbus is due and you want to finish early, then omit the following 5.5km (3.5 miles) low-level walk back to Chop Gate.)

Follow the road only until a farm access road on the left is signposted as a public footpath. Cross a bridge over the River Seph to reach **Low Mill** and note the old mill and its race. Pass between the buildings and turn right as marked, then go through a gate as marked, walking gently up alongside a field. Go through a gate and keep

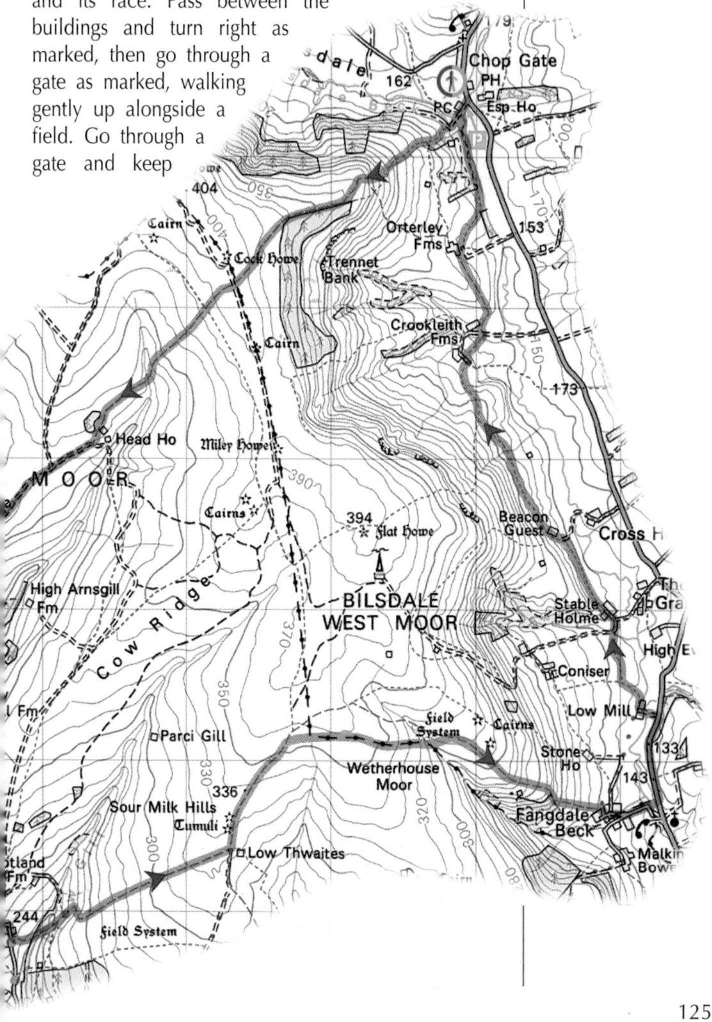

A view encompassing the moorlands, woodlands and fields of upper Ryedale

right alongside another field. Go through another gate and turn right along an access road. Branch left between the farm buildings at **Stable Holme** and keep left up a short, overgrown track.

Go through a gate and simply walk straight across a slope, following a path that can be churned up by cattle. Walk up the access road to **Beacon Guest**, which offers accommodation, and continue over a stile to walk along an overgrown path. To keep on course, bear in mind that you should always have a drystone wall on your right. The path later climbs uphill across a field to go through a gate, then you walk downhill and swing left to find a track leading through gates towards **Crookleith Farms**. Avoid the farms by walking straight down through a field as marked from a gate, and turn right to find a footbridge over a little beck. Cross and turn left, then quickly right, using tracks signposted as a bridleway. Turn right again as signposted at a house and walk alongside a field. Turn left and walk uphill alongside a field, and keep going straight over a rise to reach **Orterley Farms**.

Turn right in the farmyard, go through a gate, then turn left and cross a ladder stile. Proceed as marked through fields, but bear in mind that it can be very wet and muddy down beside the river. If that proves to be the case, then traverse a little further up the slope. Eventually turn right across a wooden bridge to return to the car park and toilets at **Chop Gate**. If food and drink are required, then head a short way up the road to the Buck Inn.

WALK 25
Chop Gate, Tripsdale, Bransdale and Bilsdale

Distance	18km (11 miles), or 13km (8 miles) using the Moorsbus service back from Fangdale Beck
Start/finish	Chop Gate car park, Bilsdale, GR 558993
Maps	OS Landranger 100; OS Explorer OL26 South
Terrain	A tough walk, mostly along clear moorland paths and tracks, but some stretches are virtually untrodden; the high moors are exposed, but low-level field paths are used from farm to farm later in the day
Refreshments	Buck Inn at Chop Gate
Transport	Regular Moorsbus services pass Chop Gate and Fangdale Beck, linking with Helmsley, Stokesley and Guisborough, and there is an occasional Moorsbus services between Chop Gate and Osmotherley

Starting from Chop Gate at the head of Bilsdale, this walk crosses hidden wooded Tripsdale, traverses the empty moors above Bransdale, then heads back to Bilsdale. It explores the broad and bleak expanse of Bilsdale East Moor, and while most paths and tracks are clear, some short stretches are rather vague. After descending to Bilsdale the route wanders from farm to farm on the valley sides to return to Chop Gate. This low-level stretch could be omitted if you land on the road near Fangdale Beck in time to catch one of the Moorsbus services.

Leave the car park at Chop Gate and turn right to walk along the **B1257**. There is a public footpath signpost on the left, close to the access road for **Esp House**. Walk diagonally up through a field, then turn left up the access road for **William Beck Farm**. Turn right in front of the house, then right again along a short grassy track to a gate. Turn left up a sunken walled grassy track to reach another gate. Walk straight up a field and go through yet another gate, then follow a narrow path up a bracken slope and continue up a heather slope on **Black Intake**. Go through one last gate and follow the path uphill to reach a clear track.

Trodden paths and tracks on **Nab End Moor** do not match the courses of rights of way on the map. The best thing to do is to turn right along the track, then left, and walk in sweeping zigzags down into the wooded recesses of **Tripsdale**. Cross a culvert bridge over Tripsdale Beck and climb steeply uphill following the zigzag track. The track straightens out and gradually levels out on the way across **Slape Wath Moor**. Keep right, which is in effect straight ahead, at a track junction, and pass close to a couple of wooden huts on the moor. Keep following the track very gently uphill, keep straight ahead at another track junction, then look out for **Stump Cross** on the right, which is an old broken marker cross set in a stone socket.

The track runs almost to 420m (1380ft) along **Bransdale Ridge**, with good views down into the lovely Bransdale. Follow the track gently downhill on the heather moorland to reach a barrier gate and minor road. Only a few paces along the road a public footpath sign points right across a moorland with the curious name of **Botany Bay**. Follow a very narrow trodden path through the heather, passing a **boundary stone** bearing the letters K and H. Follow the path down to the corner of a drystone wall, then keep right of the wall and follow it down to a little beck called **Bonfield Gill**. There are masses of squelchy rushes here, but look for a slab of rock to assist a launch across the stream on a firm footing.

Walk uphill alongside another drystone wall to reach a **stand of pines** at a corner of the wall. Climb straight uphill along a rather vague path and cross a clear track. Forge ever-upwards at a gentle gradient on the moor, but watch for the line of the path by spotting a series of **small cairns**. Eventually there are views over the broad heathery crest into Bilsdale. When a **track** is joined the continuation of the path is both vague and rugged around **Black Holes**. It is better to

129

The broken-shafted Stump Cross is passed high on heathery Bransdale Moor

turn right along the track, then turn left and follow it down the moorland slope. There are some very good views of Bilsdale on the descent.

Drop down to the right along a trodden path and go through a gate in a wall. Walk downhill through two fields and go through a couple of gates that are fairly close together. Aim as if for the head of Bilsdale, walking down a grassy slope and keeping a fence to your left. Go through a couple more gates and continue walking alongside a fence. Another gate leads into a wood where the path runs down through a very deep-cut groove. It can be wet and muddy towards the bottom, where a gate gives way to the **B1257**.

Turn left along the road, but only as far as the access road to **Low Mill**, on the right, which is sign-posted as a public footpath. (Alternatively, if a Moorsbus is due, then the final 5km (3 miles) of the route can be omitted.) Cross a bridge over the River Seph to reach Low Mill, and note the old mill and its race. Pass between the buildings and turn right as marked, then go through a gate as marked, walking gently up alongside a field. Go through a gate and keep right alongside another field. Go through another gate and turn right along an access road. Branch left between the farm buildings at **Stable Holme** and keep left up a short, overgrown track.

Go through a gate and simply walk straight across a slope, following a path that can be churned up by cattle. Walk up the access road to **Beacon Guest**, which offers accommodation, and continue over a stile to walk along an overgrown path. To keep on course, bear in mind that you should always have a drystone wall on your right. The path later climbs uphill across a field to go through a gate, then you walk downhill and swing left to find a track leading through gates towards **Crookleith Farms**. Avoid the farms by walking straight down through a field as marked from a gate, and turn right to find a footbridge over a little beck. Cross and turn left, then quickly right, using tracks signposted as a bridleway. Turn right again as signposted at a house and walk alongside a field. Turn left and walk uphill alongside a field, and keep going straight over a rise to reach **Orterley Farms**.

Turn right in the farmyard, go through a gate, then turn left and cross a ladder stile. Proceed as marked through fields, but bear in mind that it can be very wet and muddy down beside the river. If that proves to be the case, then traverse a little further up the slope. Eventually turn right across a wooden bridge to return to the car park and toilets at **Chop Gate**. If food and drink are required, then head a short way up the road to the Buck Inn.

A fine view of upper Bilsdale can be enjoyed on the descent from the moors

WALK 26
Low Mill, Harland, Rudland Rigg and West Gill

Distance	16km (10 miles)
Start/finish	Low Mill, Farndale, GR 672952
Maps	OS Landrangers 94 or 100; OS Explorer OL26 South
Terrain	A moderate but long walk; field paths are followed by a climb onto a moorland slope and across rough pasture; firm, clear stony tracks lead across the high moors, and a rugged path is used for the descent; the high moors are exposed
Refreshments	None on the route – Feversham Arms and Daffy Café off-route at Church Houses
Transport	The Farndale Daffodil bus serves Low Mill from Hutton-le-Hole in spring, and some services run through the summer

Rudland Rigg is a long and sprawling moorland to the west of Farndale. A rough stony road runs along its crest, and this could be followed all the way through the North York Moors from Gillamoor to Kildale, taking walkers over some of the highest moors with relative ease. Walkers traversing Rudland Rigg will notice dozens of curious humps and bumps, and these are the remains of bell pits where poor-quality coal was dug from the bedrock. On this walk it takes time to reach Rudland Rigg, but walkers will find that the rest of the day unfolds rapidly as good tracks are used on the high moors.

Start at **Low Mill**, where there are toilets in a car park and a post office shop across the road. Walk down the road and cross a bridge, then climb straight up the road as signposted for Gillamoor. The road eventually bends left, at which point you leave it as signposted along a public footpath through the garden of a house. Walk straight up a field to a higher house and cross a tarmac road. Walk up through another field to reach a gate leading into a wood, where there are good views around Farndale. Go through a gate at the top of the wood and turn left. Walk up a path in a groove, known as **Petergate**, on a slope of bracken, heather and bilberry. The path runs roughly along a break of slope between the higher moors and steep dale sides, passing some old stone **quarries**. Watch carefully for the line of the path, which is very narrow, flanked with heather, and cannot be easily seen looking ahead. Walk towards a patch of mixed woodland called **Cross Plantation**, then gradually swing right away from it, keeping well away from a fence seen ahead.

The path crosses a moorland track, and most of the time there is no objection to walkers turning right to follow it straight towards **Rudland Rigg**. However, the route simply steps across the track to reach the corner of a drystone wall. A farm can be seen ahead in a gentle valley, so walk down towards it, alongside the wall, crossing a ladder stile and going down through fields. Keep to the left of the farm buildings at **Harland**, then turn left along the access track to reach a neighbouring farm. Turn right and go through a gate between the farm-

house and a corrugated barn. Walk down through a field and go through another gate as marked. Keep going through fields, swinging left to walk parallel to Harland Beck. Watch carefully for a gate on the right giving access to the beck and a **footbridge**. Cross over the beck and follow a clear grassy path out of a tumbled, drystone-walled enclosure and go through another gate. Follow a heathery path that can be squelchy in places, then a wooded path to reach a small gate and a minor road.

Turn right to follow the road gently uphill, passing a building that was formerly a chapel. The road crosses a **cattle-grid** to reach open moorland. When the road turns left and heads towards Bransdale, keep straight ahead and walk gradually uphill along a stony track flanked by heather moorland. There are a couple of patches of tarmac, as well as places where the track is worn down to bedrock that looks curiously like stone paving. Later, look out for a multitude of humps and bumps which are the remains of **old bell pits**, where poor-quality coal was wrested from the ground.

Towards the top of the track you could branch left to reach a trig point on **Rudland Rigg**, at an altitude of 376m (1234ft). There are good views around the High Moors, and you can see the old road snaking onwards along the moorland crest. Follow the track very gently downhill, crossing a slight dip at **West Gill Head** where there are paths leading off to either side at 355m (1165ft). Turn right at this point to begin the descent.

A rutted path leads down past a series of bilberry-covered grouse-shooting butts. Watch out for a cairn and swing right to follow the path to a solitary **rowan tree** on the bracken, heather and bilberry moorland slope. There are a couple of marker posts, then the path descends steep and rugged for a while, becoming a fine grassy ribbon later. Go down through a gate in a wall, then turn left downhill as signposted. Go through another gate in another wall and walk down to **West Gill Beck** to cross a footbridge. Turn right through a gate and go through another gate to follow a clear grassy track past derelict **High Barn**. Keep to the track, through more gates, to pass **Horn End** farm and leave by following its gravel access track downhill. When a minor road is reached, simply turn right to walk back into the little village of **Low Mill**.

FARNDALE DAFFODILS

Walkers who visit Farndale in spring should consider walking the easy riverside path between Low Mill and Church Houses, which links Walk 26 and Walk 27. The Farndale Nature Reserve, normally green and grassy, turns into a mass of yellow when the wild daffodils are in bloom. Visitors have made their way to Farndale for decades to enjoy this spectacle, and in the past many would pick a bunch, or even scythe them for collection and ultimate sale! Since 1955 the daffodils have been protected, and they are jealously guarded today – anyone caught picking them can be fined £5!

WALK 27
Church Houses, Bloworth Crossing and Farndale Moor

Distance	20km (12.5 miles)
Start/finish	Church Houses, Farndale, GR 669975
Maps	OS Landranger 94; OS Explorer OL26 South and North
Terrain	A moderate but long moorland walk; minor roads give way to clear, firm, easy tracks across the moors; the high moors are exposed
Refreshments	Feversham Arms at Church Houses, the Daffy Café is off-route at High Mill, and the Lion Inn is off-route at Blakey
Transport	The Farndale Daffodil bus serves Church Houses and Low Mill from Hutton-le-Hole in spring, and some services run through summer; regular Moorsbus services pass a road junction on Blakey Ridge, offering links with Danby, Pickering and Helmsley

Farndale is quite charming, while the moors that flank it are quite bleak and barren. However, the High Moors are also served by a loose network of tracks that allows walkers to eat up the distance while striding out along firm, dry and gently graded surfaces. Apart from the initial steep climb, this walk is actually quite easy, and route-finding is relatively simple too, but bear in mind that the moors are exposed in bad weather and shelter is very limited. This walk makes a fine circuit high around the head of Farndale from the tiny village of Church Houses, though walkers could also easily start and finish from the Moorsbus bus stop at the junction on Blakey Ridge instead.

Start at **Church Houses** near the head of Farndale, where the Feversham Arms offers food, drink and accommodation. Set off along a road signposted 'Farndale (West Side)', walking downhill to cross a bridge, then climbing steeply to a road junction. Turn right, as signposted for

Dale End, to reach **Monket House**. Turn left as signposted for Bransdale from a gate. Follow a concrete road uphill through another gate, then climb up past a couple of bare humps of shale. Keep following a gravel track up a slope of heather, bracken and bilberry, and keep straight ahead at junctions with other tracks. At a higher level there is more heather cover and the track levels out. Reach a cross-tracks at **Ouse Gill Head**, at 369m (1211ft), then turn right.

Simply follow a broad clear track gently uphill and across the high moors. Of particular interest along the way are a series of old marker stones bearing curious placename spellings. Look out first for a stone on the right marking the 'Kirby Rode'. Keep to the track, passing intersections with footpaths and bridleways, and note broken **Cockam Cross** well off to the left, marking 'Stoxli Rode' and 'Brans Dale'. Later, the chunky **Cammon Stone** is on the right. The track rolls along across the moors, and you should keep straight ahead and avoid a couple of tracks leading off to the left. Pass a leaning stone that declares the way to 'Kirby Moor Sid', then a few paces lead up to an intersection of tracks at **Bloworth Crossing**, at 388m (1273ft). The Cleveland Way runs to the left and straight ahead, but our route around the head of Farndale turns right.

The chunky Cammon Stone is passed along the track to Bloworth Crossing

Pass a barrier gate to walk along the trackbed of the former Rosedale Railway. (See Walk 30 and Walk 31 for historical notes about the old line.) First walk along a low embankment, then pass through a shallow cutting as the track curves left. Cross a moorland beck on a little embankment, then the cutting at **Middle Head** can be a bit wet and muddy. The track curves and crosses another little embankment across another moorland beck, and enjoys fine views over Farndale from **Dale Head**. Gentle curves give way to a long low embankment which slips over the moorland crest, so that you look down into Westerdale for a change. There is a junction with a clear track that leads down into the dale, but keep straight ahead.

The old railway trackbed rises very gently and overlooks Farndale again from **Farndale Moor**. On the way uphill there are more curves, then suddenly, as a shallow cutting is reached, the Lion Inn can be seen on a moorland crest across a valley. The trackbed makes a great curve around the valley and the inn passes from sight, but it can be reached by making a short detour along a path up to the left. Staying on the trackbed, however, a gate and a road junction are soon reached on **Blakey Ridge**.

Moorsbus services can be intercepted at this road junction, but the return to Farndale is simple and straightforward. Turn right and follow the road steeply downhill, as signposted for Farndale, and the moorland slopes give way to rough pastures and green fields. Simply keep walking straight ahead to return to **Church Houses** and the Feversham Arms.

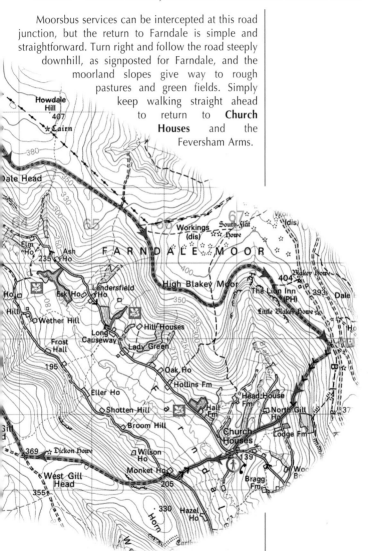

WALK 28
Hutton le Hole, Ana Cross, Spaunton Moor and Lastingham

Distance	13km (8 miles)
Start/finish	Ryedale Folk Museum, Hutton-le-Hole, GR 705900
Maps	OS Landranger 94 or 100; OS Explorer OL26 South
Terrain	A moderate moorland walk where paths need care at first, being vague in places; good tracks are used later, and paths towards the end are good too; the high moors are exposed
Refreshments	Pubs and tea rooms at Hutton-le-Hole, pubs at Lastingham
Transport	Regular Moorsbus services to Hutton-le-Hole from Pickering and Helmsley; Lastingham has occasional Hutchinsons bus services

Hutton-le-Hole is a charming village that spans a stream and sits where the Tabular Hills give way to the high heather expanses in the heart of the North York Moors. Take care over route-finding on the initial ascent, as paths are rather vague and it is all too easy to be drawn off along clearer tracks. The top of Spaunton Moor is crowned with Ana Cross, and from that point a clear track descends directly towards Lastingham. The village can be explored, or walkers can simply head straight back along a low-level series of paths to return to Hutton-le-Hole and the splendid Ryedale Folk Museum.

Leave **Hutton-le-Hole** by taking the road signposted for Lastingham, passing a car park and toilets on the edge of the village. A little further up the road, turn left along a grassy track and go through a gate. Follow the obvious grassy path gently uphill on a heather moorland slope. Turn left later along narrow **Lodge Road**, and follow it until a sign is reached at **Wheat Lund** announcing that the continuation to Spaunton Lodge is private. Turn right to leave the road and follow another clear grassy track up

A view of Hutton-le-Hole and the moorland slopes of Spaunton Moor beyond

the broad heather moorland crest of **Hutton Ridge**. Watch carefully to spot a narrower path branching to the right of the track, but essentially pursuing a parallel line. This is the right of way, though if you follow the other track by mistake, you can correct yourself later by turning right along a clearer track. The path joins this clearer track and turns right itself at 250m (820ft).

Follow the track gently down the heather moor to cross a beck. The track rises and falls towards another beck, but turn left before reaching it, and ford it near a stone **sheep-fold** where the ground is wet and boggy. Continue up through a firm grassy space on the heather moor and keep following a path to reach a road at a public footpath signpost. Turn left and walk up the road at a gentle gradient to reach **Chimney Bank** at 312m (1024ft), then turn right along a clear track from a barrier gate. There should be no mistaking the landmark **Ana Cross**, reached by branching right from the track, as it stands on a tumulus on top of **Spaunton Moor** over 290m (950ft).

Follow a clear and obvious track due south from Ana Cross. Keep right at a junction of tracks and keep walking straight downhill. In fact, simply keep to the broadest and clearest track on the moorland slope, passing **Spring**

Heads until the stony surface finally gives way to a grassy one. There is a millennium stone beside a junction of paths just before the track reaches a gate. The village of **Lastingham** can be explored by going down through the gate and returning to this point later. The route, however, turns right.

Ana Cross is a prominent moorland marker planted high on Spaunton Moor

LASTINGHAM

This little village is huddled between the Tabular Hills and High Moors and can easily be explored by making a detour down from the route. Of particular interest is St Mary's Church, with its Norman crypt and Shrine of St Cedd, originally built in 1078 on the site of an ancient Celtic monastery. Food and drink are available from the Blacksmith's Arms and Lastingham Grange Hotel.

Turn right and follow a wall down into a valley where the ground near **Hole Beck** is wet enough to support bog myrtle. Ford the beck and climb up the other side, then follow a grassy track alongside the wall. Marker posts show the way across a grassy slope well above **Camomile Farm**, then you continue along a grassy track alongside a fence. This eventually swings left and goes through a gate to reach a minor road. Turn right along the road and later keep a lookout for a grassy track forking left, signposted as a public footpath. Go through a gate and follow a woodland path down to a **footbridge**, cross over it, then follow the path as marked through fields to return to **Hutton-le-Hole**. The path pops out onto the road at the village hall. Turn right to return to the **Ryedale Folk Museum**.

HUTTON-LE-HOLE

Hutton-le-Hole has a long history of settlement dating back to Neolithic times. The village was mentioned in the Domesday Book as 'Hoton', but throughout the ages it has also been rendered as 'Hege-Hoton', 'Hoton under Heg', and 'Hewton'. As a placename 'Hutton-le-Hole' dates only from the 19th century. The village features the Ryedale Folk Museum, Barn Hotel, Crown Inn and a couple of tea shops and gift shops.

RYEDALE FOLK MUSEUM

Trace the history of Yorkshire folk from 4000 BC to 1953, with plenty of hands-on exhibits, as you wander from one part of the museum site to another. Over a dozen buildings have been erected since 1964, some with roofs supported by enormous cruck frames (curved timbers), some standing in isolation, while others are arranged as a row of small shops. Vintage vehicles, including motorised and horse-drawn carriages, are preserved. Land around the site sprouts vegetables and flowers, including many varieties of cornfield flowers. Local folk often give demonstrations of traditional crafts while wearing period dress. There is an entrance charge, and the museum incorporates a shop, toilets and tourist information centre, ☎ 01751 417367.

WALK 29
Rosedale Abbey, Hartoft, Lastingham and Ana Cross

Distance	14km (8.75 miles)
Start/finish	Rosedale Abbey, GR 724959
Maps	OS Landranger 94 or 100; OS Explorer OL26 South and OL27 South
Terrain	A moderate moorland walk where farm roads give way to rugged paths that can be muddy in places; moorland paths and tracks become firmer later, and the high moors are exposed
Refreshments	Pubs and tea rooms around Rosedale Abbey, pubs at Lastingham
Transport	Occasional Moorsbus and Hutchinson's bus services to Rosedale Abbey from Pickering

Rosedale is a charming pastoral dale, but explorers don't need to climb too far up the valley sides to discover wild and rugged slopes. This route wanders along the valley side from the neat stone village of Rosedale Abbey to pass Hartoft on a rugged moorland slope. Staying on the moorland fringe, the route passes close enough to Lastingham for a quick visit to be possible, then climbs over the top of Spaunton Moor to reach Ana Cross. A rapid descent leads back to Rosedale Abbey via Rosedale Chimney Bank.

Leave the village green at **Rosedale Abbey** and follow the road signposted for Pickering. Turn right before the **Coach House Inn** to follow a narrow road signposted for Thorgill. A sign warns motorists of 1:3 gradients on **Rosedale Chimney Bank**, but walkers don't climb that far. Turn left at the White Horse Farm Hotel, along a clear track passing a couple of farmhouse bed and breakfasts. The track ends at **Hollins Farm**, but just before reaching the farm turn right, as signposted along a bridleway, up a grassy track. (Follow the path beside the drystone wall, not the path climbing straight up the moorland slope.)

The path leads through bracken, at first fairly close to the wall, then it drifts further away and further uphill from the wall. It contours across a slope of bracken and heather, passing below curiously named **Cumratph Crag**. Watch out for a cast-iron plaque marking the point where in Elizabethan times there was a glass furnace, for which Rosedale was once famous. Eventually the path rises from bracken slopes to heather moorland above **Hartoft**, though the moor is cut with great swathes of bilberry and cowberry too. Descend to the corner of a drystone wall and continue straight ahead beside it. There are a few trees around here, and a farm access track is joined near **High Askew**. Follow the track uphill away from the farm.

At the top of the track watch for a grassy track forking to the right through the heather. Follow this until it intersects with another grassy track. Turn left, then after a few paces turn right and approach a drystone wall. Turn right to follow the wall downhill, then head straight down to ford **Tranmire Beck**. Climb uphill and continue along a grassy track with a wall and fields to the left and open moorland to the right. After crossing a rise follow the track down to an intersection of

A view of Rosedale taking in the countryside on the way to Hollins Farm

paths and tracks beside a millennium stone near **Lastingham**. The village is close enough to be easily visited and explored. (See Walk 28 for facilities and points of interest.)

Turn right to follow a grassy track uphill, and it soon becomes a broad and stony track on a wide heather moorland. Follow the track past **Spring Heads** and keep climbing gently. Keep left at a junction of tracks and aim straight for the landmark **Ana Cross** on the horizon, standing on a tumulus on top of **Spaunton Moor** over 290m (950ft). Walk past the cross and turn left along another broad and clear track. This leads to a barrier gate and a minor road at **Chimney Bank**, at 312m (1024ft).

Most walkers will be happy to turn right and follow the road straight downhill to return to Rosedale Abbey, but most of the road can be avoided as follows. Walk a short way down the road and turn left at a small car park. Follow a gravel path past some stone arches and continue above **Bank Top cottages**. Turn right to walk just a short way down the access road, then keep left of three trees, well away from the cottages. Follow a vague grooved path, which becomes a clearer grassy groove bending left downhill. Continue down a narrow path on a steep slope of bracken, crossing stiles and turning right and left as marked on the little **Red House Golf Course**. Cross a narrow road and walk straight down through a field to reach a road beside a house. Cross a bridge and walk straight back into the village of **Rosedale Abbey**.

147

WALK 30
Rosedale Ironstone Railway around Rosedale Head

Distance	19km (12 miles)
Start/finish	Rosedale Abbey, GR 724959
Maps	OS Landranger 94; OS Explorer OL26 South and OL26 North
Terrain	An easy but long walk, mostly on a firm and level moorland track, though field paths at the start and finish can be steep and muddy in places
Refreshments	Pubs and tea rooms at Rosedale Abbey, and the Lion Inn is off-route at Blakey
Transport	Occasional Moorsbus and Hutchinson's bus services to Rosedale Abbey from Pickering, and regular Moorsbus services run along Blakey Ridge

The Rosedale Ironstone Railway ran from 1861 to 1926 so that large deposits of ironstone could be stripped from the high moors. Some initial processing of the ore was carried out in massive stone kilns, and trains pulled up to 15 loaded wagons at a time along the line around the head of Rosedale and away to Middlesbrough. The old trackbed running high around Rosedale can easily be made into a circular walk by using paths to climb up to it and descend from it, starting and finishing in the village of Rosedale Abbey. The old railway trackbed runs anywhere from 250m to 370m (820ft to 1215ft), but is so gently graded that in effect it contours around the dale.

Leave the village green at **Rosedale Abbey** and follow the road signposted for Pickering. Turn right before the **Coach House Inn** to follow a narrow road signposted for Thorgill. A sign warns motorists of 1:3 gradients on **Rosedale Chimney Bank**. Walkers can use the road if they wish, but there is a different way uphill along paths. Follow the road across a bridge, then take a footpath

The Rosedale Ironstone Railway seen at the top of Rosedale Chimney Bank

straight uphill from a house, through a field, to cross another minor road. Walk up onto the little **Red House Golf Course** and turn right and left as marked, over ladder stiles and left again up a steep slope of bracken. Follow a grassy groove up a heather moorland slope and swing right to pass three trees well to the right of **Bank Top cottages**. Follow the access track uphill, away from the cottages, to link with the old railway trackbed. Consider making a short detour left along a gravel path to see a set of eight **stone arches** where ironstone was roasted before being loaded onto railway wagons. The altitude of the trackbed at this point is around 300m (985ft). A chimney stood nearby until 1972, hence the name **Rosedale Chimney Bank**.

Double back and follow the old railway trackbed from a barrier gate, enjoying fine views over Rosedale. Pass a **wooden bench** and follow the stony or cinder track across a moorland slope of heather and bilberry. The trackbed makes a big loop around **Thorgill Head**, then passes a crumbling ruin at **Sheriff's Pit**. Keep going through a shallow cutting, though the trackbed is generally perched on a moorland edge overlooking Rosedale. Later a sign points left for **Blakey Bank**, around 370m (1215ft), if any walkers wish to switch to Walk 31, otherwise keep straight ahead. (There used to be a few cottages nearby, housing railway workers.) Pass a barrier gate and cross a track, and later there are two signposts pointing up to the left for the Lion Inn at **Blakey**, well-placed for a lunch break, especially on a wild day.

Keep following the cinder trackbed across heather moorland slopes, passing a brick wall with an arched window. The trackbed is on a raised embankment as it swings right to cross the headwaters of the River Seven at **Rosedale Head**. Some parts of the track are a bit muddy, and one boggy cutting is best avoided by using a path above it.

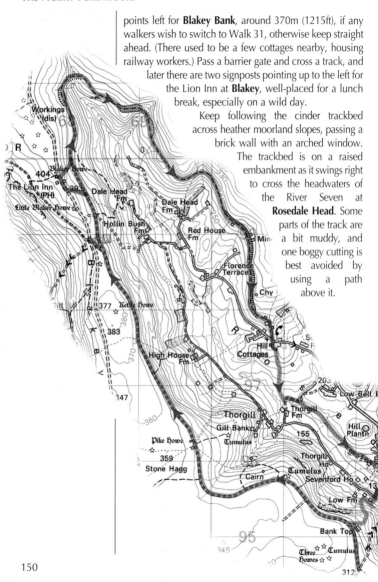

BLAKEY

Blakey is a bleak spot, but food, drink and accommodation are offered at the celebrated Lion Inn, at over 400m (1315ft). The inn was once popular with the coal and ironstone miners who worked on the moors, and is popular today with walkers and motorists. Accommodation is also available across the road at High Blakey House, where paths leading to and from the old railway are signposted at either side. (Regular Moorsbus services link the inn with Danby, Helmsley and Pickering, offering an alternative start.)

Cross another curved embankment at **Reeking Gill**, then follow an easier and firmer stretch of the old line. Another cutting is firm, dry and grassy, followed by another embankment at **Nab Scar**. Go round another curved embankment and follow a broad and grassy stretch of the old trackbed, but avoid spurs rising to the left. Pass a small ruin and four big crumbling stone buttresses. Next, pass below a chimney stump and **16 stone arches** where ironstone was once roasted. Keep left of the last crumbling buildings, the remains of a once-busy area known as the Depots, to go through a gate. Follow a track down to **Hill Cottages**.

Cross a minor road and continue down another track signposted as a public footpath. Go through a kissing gate and walk down beside a field, then go through another kissing gate and walk straight down through a couple of fields to follow a stone-paved path. Do not cross a footbridge near **Low Thorgill Farm**, but turn left to walk downstream beside the **River Seven**. Follow a track that can be muddy, but when it climbs away from the river watch for a path marked off to the right. Look for more markers and stiles to proceed downstream through fields and a wood before climbing away from the river to later follow an access road through a **caravan site**. (Bear in mind that facilities on the site are private.) Also watch out for a glimpse of a little **church** on the left, then turn left to follow a short path out of the site. Walk through the churchyard to return to the village green in the middle of **Rosedale Abbey**.

151

ROSEDALE ABBEY

Only a small section of spiral stairway remains of the original 12th-century Cistercian nunnery, though the church occupies the same site. Facilities around the village include the Milburn Arms Hotel, Coach House Inn, Rosedale Bakery and General Stores, and the Abbey Stores and Tea Room. There is a car park and toilets. A glass workshop brings the process of glass-making back to Rosedale after an absence of several centuries!

View across Rosedale from the old railway trackbed to the Lion Inn at Blakey

WALK 31
Rosedale Ironstone Railway from Blakey to Battersby

Distance	17km (10.5 miles)
Start	Blakey Bank, Blakey Ridge, GR 683989
Finish	Battersby Junction, GR 588072
Maps	OS Landrangers 93 and 94; OS Explorers OL26 South and OL26 North
Terrain	Easy walking along a clear firm trackbed across high moors and down through forest; minor roads are used at the end
Refreshments	The Lion Inn is close to the start on Blakey Ridge, the Dudley Arms is off-route at Ingleby Greenhow near the end
Transport	Regular Moorsbus services along Blakey Ridge from Danby, Helmsley and Pickering, and Arriva trains run regularly from Battersby Junction to Whitby and Middlesbrough

After iron ore had been mined and roasted around Rosedale, trains carried up to 15 loaded wagons at a time away from the dale, around the head of Farndale. The wagons were divided into threes to be lowered down a 1:5 incline from the moors. The men who lived and worked on the moors at the top of the incline referred to their workplace as Siberia! The whole of the old railway line around Rosedale, as well as to Battersby Junction, is available for walkers and cyclists, while horse-riders can apply for a permit to use it. As this is a linear route, walkers should use the Moorsbus to reach Blakey, then link with one of the Arriva trains when they reach Battersby Junction.

Start at a road junction on **Blakey Bank**, around 370m (1215ft), which is also close to the junction of the old railway trackbeds. Under the road a blocked tunnel can be discerned, where the railway passed from Rosedale to Farndale, and there is a parking space beside the road overlooking the old junction. The road signposted down

153

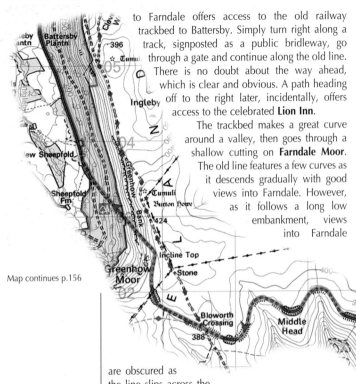

Map continues p.156

to Farndale offers access to the old railway trackbed to Battersby. Simply turn right along a track, signposted as a public bridleway, go through a gate and continue along the old line. There is no doubt about the way ahead, which is clear and obvious. A path heading off to the right later, incidentally, offers access to the celebrated **Lion Inn**.

The trackbed makes a great curve around a valley, then goes through a shallow cutting on **Farndale Moor**. The old line features a few curves as it descends gradually with good views into Farndale. However, as it follows a long low embankment, views into Farndale are obscured as the line slips across the moorland crest, and the head of Westerdale is seen instead. Views into Farndale are restored later, and the trackbed begins to curve again around **Dale Head**. A curved length of embankment crosses a moorland beck, then a cutting at **Middle Head** can be a bit wet and muddy. Cross another moorland beck on another curved embankment, then go through a shallow cutting. A low embankment leads to a barrier gate and a prominent inter-section of tracks at **Bloworth Crossing**, at 388m (1273ft).

The Cleveland Way is signposted straight ahead and to the right. Follow the old trackbed straight ahead and pass another barrier gate. The Cleveland Way later heads off to

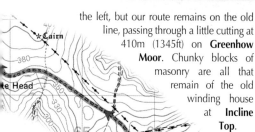

the left, but our route remains on the old line, passing through a little cutting at 410m (1345ft) on **Greenhow Moor**. Chunky blocks of masonry are all that remain of the old winding house at **Incline Top**.

The view down into Farndale from the old Rosedale Ironstone Railway

Wagons used to be unhitched from their engines at this point and lowered in relays to engines at the bottom of the slope, which has a gradient of 1:5. Simply walk straight down the old incline, which drops rapidly from the moorland, passing through a gate to enter a forest, then swinging right at the bottom to continue on a level at 140m (460ft).

A gate later leads out of the forest, passing a few cottages, with views of the Cleveland Hills off to the left. However, the dirt road is still well wooded and at times views are quite limited. **Battersby Plantation** stands to the right, almost all the way to a junction with a farm road at **Bank Foot**. The last part of the old line cannot be followed, as it has been lost among fields. Turn left gently up the road to reach a junction, then turn right as signposted for the station. Walk along the road and turn left for **Battersby Junction**, timing your arrival to suit one of the trains running towards Whitby or Middlesbrough. (If you find you are far too early for a train, then consider a detour to the nearby village of **Ingleby Greenhow**, where the Dudley Arms offers food and drink.)

Continued
from p.154

The 1:5 incline trackbed drops straight from the High Moors to the low plains

WALK 32
Westerdale, Fat Betty, Westerdale Moor and Esklets

Distance	15km (9.5 miles)
Start/finish	Parish church, Westerdale, GR 664058
Maps	OS Landranger 94; OS Explorer OL26 North
Terrain	A tough walk along farm tracks, field paths and moorland paths; a stretch of road is used on the high moors, then paths used on the descent need care, being vague in places, and possibly wet and muddy; the high moors are exposed
Refreshments	None on the route, but available well off-route at Castleton and Blakey
Transport	None to Westerdale, but regular Moorsbus services run over the higher moors to and from Danby, Helmsley and Pickering

The village of Westerdale, and indeed the dale itself, has the air of being well off the beaten track – perhaps more walkers and cyclists visited it when Westerdale Hall Youth Hostel was in operation. There is no public transport into the dale, but anyone relying on public transport can easily restructure the walk to start high on the moors where Moorsbus services run. Starting from Westerdale, however, this walk climbs gradually to the High Moors, taking in sundry boundary stones and stone crosses, then descends to Esklets for a long walk back through the dale, passing farms and cottages.

Leave the parish church in the lovely little village of **Westerdale** and follow the road uphill to reach a junction at a house called **Pinfold**. Turn left along a road, then *either* turn right at a gate, as signposted public footpath, *or* walk down to a crossroads and turn right along another road, which the path quickly joins in any case. Either way, the road runs to **Broad Gate Farm** where the Westerdale Bunk Barn is located, and ice creams may be available from a house!

Walk straight past the farm and continue through gates and alongside fields, then veer left as signposted along a bridleway to cross **Tower Beck**. Climb up a short wooded slope and walk up alongside a field to find a way to the farm at **Dale Head**. Pass by the buildings as directed and admire the fine old stonework. Go through a gate onto a moorland slope and follow a grooved path uphill. This becomes a grassy groove on a heathery slope, but the

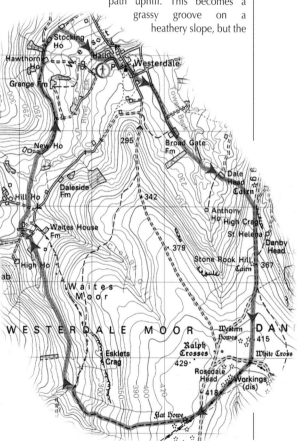

moorland magic is lost as it reaches a road junction on **Castleton Rigg**, over 330m (1085ft). Looking back across Westerdale from this point you can spot the prominent peak of Roseberry Topping.

Turn right to walk up the road and note the **boundary stones** arranged in a sparse line to the right, each one with a whitewashed top. Walk up the road, and watch for it bending to the right, so that the boundary stones are suddenly arranged on the left. Follow a narrow moorland path from stone to stone through the heather, reaching the distinctive moorland marker **Fat Betty**, also known as the White Cross, over 410m (1345ft). Money may have been deposited on the stone for needy travellers. Step across a nearby road as signposted along a public bridleway, and veer to the right along a narrow path running gently down through the heather. Pass spoil heaps from old bell pits, as well as a boundary stone, then the path bottoms out and climbs gently, passing another boundary stone to reach a road at **Rosedale Head**.

Fat Betty, or the White Cross, is surely the most distinctive moorland marker

Cross the road and pass **Margery Bradley Stone** to follow a track away from the road. The track is clear and obvious, but keep right at a junction at **Flat Howe**, over 420m (1380ft), and continue onwards until only a vague path leads past some grouse-shooting butts. Keep an eye open to spot a yellow-painted post, as the path is quite indistinct beyond the butts. The next feature to spot on the way down **Westerdale Moor** is a yellow-painted stile over a fence. From that point drop more steeply down onto a grassier moorland shelf. Go through a gateway in a drystone wall and watch for paint blobs and arrows leading off to the right down a rugged bouldery slope. Go through a gateway and walk down alongside a drystone wall, turning right at the bottom through another gateway. Cross a beck and follow a track up to another track at **Esklets**, and turn right to cross another beck.

Follow the clear track through a couple of gateways, when it becomes obvious that it is heading up to a stand on pines on a slope. Veer right as marked down a narrow grassy path and cross a step-stile. Continue down through the valley, taking care to cross a small **footbridge** hidden among trees. Follow the path uphill from the bridge at first, then continue downstream, though some distance above the beck, on the rugged slopes of **Waites Moor**. Note the rowan trees and the mosaic of vegetation types on the slopes, but keep an eye on the narrow muddy path. Yellow paint blobs occur at intervals, and later you walk alongside a woodland before moving in among the trees as marked to reach a foot-bridge and farm access road below **High House**.

Cross the bridge and bear right, soon crossing another footbridge. Keep to the left of a farm as marked, crossing stiles and a farm access road, followed by another **foot-bridge** in turn as you walk downstream through fields. Walk across a field and up through a field to reach a gate and farm access road near **New House**. Turn right to follow the road, with a drystone wall and fields down to the right and a bilberry moorland rising to the left. Continue this way until almost at **Grange Farm**, then as the track climbs towards mounds of shale spoil, veer right to go through a gate as marked. Look ahead for gateways while walking through fields, and keep to the left of the next farm buildings to follow another access road uphill from **Hawthorn House**.

Don't go too far up the farm access road, but branch right along a lesser track marked as a public footpath. Go in front of **Stocking House**, passing through gates, then once clear of the house go through a gate on the left. Continue walking ahead to reach **Brown House** and turn right into the garden. Walk straight downhill from the house, as signposted for Westerdale, through fields to cross a footbridge over the **River Esk**. Follow a track uphill, which can be muddy, then cross a pathless field to reach a gate and minor road. Turn left to follow the road past splendid **Westerdale Hall**, once a shooting lodge and youth hostel, but now a dwelling. The road leads back into the village of **Westerdale** where a right turn leads back to the parish church.

WALK 33
Danby, Castleton, Botton Village and Danby Rigg

Distance	16km (10 miles)
Start/finish	Danby Railway Station, GR 707084
Maps	OS Landranger 94; OS Explorer OL26 North
Terrain	A moderate walk along roads, tracks and paths through woods, fields and over high moors; some field paths require careful route-finding
Refreshments	Duke of Wellington and a café at Danby; Eskdale Inn, Downe Arms and tea room at Castleton; Fox and Hounds at Ainthorpe
Transport	Regular Moorsbus services to Danby from Pickering, Helmsley and Guisborough, and Arriva trains link Danby and Castleton with Whitby and Middlesbrough

This walk essentially explores the low-lying reaches of Eskdale and Danby Dale, then climbs over the high moors of Danby Rigg. The first part of the walk is a simple stroll from Danby to Castleton in Eskdale. Towards the head of Danby Dale walkers have the opportunity to visit Botton Village, operated by the Camphill Trust, and where agricultural and craft activities provide employment for over 300 people, many of them with special needs. After crossing Danby Rigg the route returns to Danby, which is a natural transport hub in the dale, with rail and Moorsbus services. The Moors Centre is within easy walking distance of the village if a visit is desired.

Leave the railway station and turn left to walk up into the village of **Danby**. The Duke of Wellington is located at a crossroads, with the post office general store and Stonehouse Bakery and Teashop nearby, along with toilets. Turn left along the road signposted for Castleton, following it uphill, downhill and uphill again. When a road junction is reached, branch right along a grassy track signposted for Castleton and the 'Esk Valley Walk'. This cuts across a bracken slope where you keep left at a couple of path junctions. Go through a gate into the wood at **Danby Park**. The wood is mostly birch and a clear path runs across the slope to exit at another gate. Follow a grassy track through a couple of gates to pass farm buildings at **Park Nook**. Walk along the access road from the farm to a road where a left turn downhill leads under the railway to pass the **Eskdale Inn**. Food, drink and accommodation are offered.

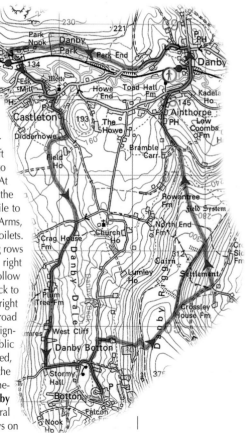

Cross a bridge over the **River Esk** and keep left to follow the road up into the village of **Castleton**. At the top of Station Road is the Castleton Tea Rooms, while to the right are the Downe Arms, post office, Co-op and toilets. Turn left downhill, passing rows of stone houses, then turn right down **Ashfield Road**. Follow the road across Danby Beck to pass Ashfield Farm. Turn right after passing the access road for **Brookfield Farm**, as signposted along a public bridleway. Walk as directed, in a loop well clear from the farmhouse, to cross a stone-slab bridge over **Danby Beck**. Go through several gates and fields, not always on

The route runs low through Danby Dale after leaving the village of Castleton

a trodden path, but look ahead to spot all the large gates with blue waymark arrows and/or Esk Valley Walk markers. Eventually a road junction will be reached.

Walk straight ahead at the junction, as marked 'No through road', and follow the road up to West Green Farm and **Plum Tree Farm**. Walk straight along a grassy track, then cross a stone step-stile to continue through fields, heading straight for **Westcliffe Farm**. Follow the access track past another nearby farm, and keep straight ahead along a farm road to reach a road junction at **Stormy Hall**. Turn left down the road and pass a little chapel at the bottom. Keep left and follow the road uphill to another junction. A right turn at this point leads quickly to **Botton Village**. If you go there, return to the junction afterwards. If you omit the village, then simply turn left to continue by road.

BOTTON VILLAGE

Botton Village is operated by the Camphill Trust. There is a car park, shops, creamery and food centre. The community is essentially based around Christian family life, and over 300 people, many with special needs, live in family houses grouped in neighbourhoods around working farms. Agriculture and craft production are the main occupations, and while no one receives a wage, everyone has a worthwhile and productive job, and a place in the community. For Camphill Trust information, ☎ 01287 661294.

If returning to the crossroads from **Botton Village** simply walk straight through to continue, then turn right up the **East Cliff** access road. Keep left of the farm as indicated, then turn right, then left to walk straight up through a field. Keep climbing and drift to the right in an enclosure full of bracken to reach a gate. Turn left through the gate, then swing right up a groove on a slope of bracken where the path can be squelchy. Drift left along a narrow path through heather on the higher slopes, passing a few small cairns on the way across **Danby Rigg**, touching 350m (1150ft). The path you follow is known as Jack Sledge Road and it leads steep and rugged down to a minor road in **Little Fryup Dale**. Keep left to walk down the road, but only to a junction. At that point turn left as signposted along a public bridleway, and follow a green ribbon of a path, steepening on the rugged hillside, until it is chiselled deep into the rock as it climbs onto the moorland brow. (Walkers will notice a path on the moorland brow avoiding the need to descend into Little Fryup Dale and climb uphill again. While not a right of way, the path is well used.)

Whichever way you reach the moorland brow, pass an **upright stone** marker and descend gently along the northern slopes of the moor, passing a larger upright stone. A gate takes the path off the heather moor and down between thick gorse bushes to land on a minor road near the **Danby Tennis Club** courts. Walk down the road and keep right, passing the Fox and Hounds at **Ainthorpe**, which offers food, drink and accommodation. At the bottom end of the village keep right as signposted for Danby, crossing a bridge over the **River Esk** to return to the railway station. Alternatively, walk back up into **Danby** and consider making a right turn to include a visit to the Moors Centre at Danby Lodge. (See Walk 23 for information about the Moors Centre.)

WALK 34
Lealholm, Heads, Glaisdale Moor and Glaisdale Rigg

Distance	22.5km (14 miles)
Start/finish	Lealholm Railway Station, Eskdale, GR 762078
Maps	OS Landranger 94; OS Explorer OL27 North
Terrain	A long and tough walk – minor roads give way to a farm track and vague hillside paths; a high moorland road gives way to clear moorland paths and tracks; the high moors are exposed, and the route finishes on minor roads
Refreshments	Board Inn and Shepherds Hall restaurant and tea rooms at Lealholm
Transport	Arriva trains serve Lealholm from Whitby and Middlesbrough

Great Fryup Dale is one of many dales that link with Eskdale. A walk around it, taking in the moorland slopes on either side, is quite lengthy. On this walk minor roads are used to cross the dale, then paths over the rugged hump of Heads can be rather vague in places. After following a road onto the high moors, the route links with the course of the celebrated Coast to Coast Walk across the head of Great Fryup Dale, and this leads in turn onto the moorland crest of Glaisdale Rigg. The route uses a moorland track and quiet country roads to return to Lealholm in Eskdale.

Leave Lealholm Railway Station by crossing the railway line and following a path straight down into **Lealholm** village, landing beside the post office with another shop across the road. Turn left, then right by road to cross an arched stone bridge over the River Esk and pass the Board Inn, which offers food, drink and accommodation. Follow the road straight uphill, passing a junction, then turn right at a higher junction, and right again downhill as signposted for Fryup each time. Keep walking down the road as signposted for Danby, then the road bottoms out and crosses a bridge over **Great Fryup Beck**. Climb straight up the road to pass Furnace Farm bed and breakfast and follow the road as it bends left. Turn right up the access track for **Head House farm**.

Keep right of the farmyard and go through a gate into a field. Walk alongside the field with a wooded slope falling away to the right. Keep straight ahead along this line, through other gates and fields, to reach a moorland slope. The route, though untrodden at this point, is along a public bridleway that technically drifts left to reach the heathery crest of **Heads** at 270m (885ft). It then drifts right and is clear underfoot as it runs back downhill. Be sure to descend along a track well to the right of the pine-clad end of the crest. Go down through a gate and along a grassy track on a slope of bracken, passing a few pines. Keep left at a fork then later turn right, through a gate, to follow a grassy track downhill between walls. Turn left at a track junction to reach a road near **Stonebeck Gate Farm**.

A fine grassy track descends towards Stonebeck Gate in Little Fryup Dale

Turn left up the road to reach a farmhouse called **Fairy Cross Plain**. Turn right through a gate, as signposted public bridleway, and head across a field to reach the only other gate in view. Go through and bear right up to another gateway. Follow a grooved path across the flank of a prominent pointed hill, continuing across a bracken slope along a narrow path to reach a gate. A groove on the moorland slope leads up to a minor road. Turn left to follow the road gently uphill on the heather crest of **Danby High Moor**. This is a spectacularly empty road, leading to a lonely gateway at 420m (1380ft) where a track on the left is signposted as a bridleway to Glaisdale. It is also waymarked as part of the Coast to Coast Walk.

Follow a clear track across the heather moor and pass the stout little stone building of **Trough House**. Keep following the clear track around the head of Great Fryup Dale, descending gently before climbing gently along a

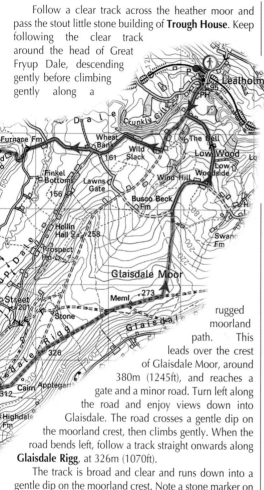

rugged moorland path. This leads over the crest of Glaisdale Moor, around 380m (1245ft), and reaches a gate and a minor road. Turn left along the road and enjoy views down into Glaisdale. The road crosses a gentle dip on the moorland crest, then climbs gently. When the road bends left, follow a track straight onwards along **Glaisdale Rigg**, at 326m (1070ft).

The track is broad and clear and runs down into a gentle dip on the moorland crest. Note a stone marker on the left where 'Gisbro' and 'Whitby Road' can be discerned among the carvings, though other names are indistinct. Avoid other tracks on either side, and follow the main track as it climbs gently uphill and downhill on

Trough House is a lonely shooting hut situated up on Danby High Moor

the slopes of **Glaisdale Moor**. A public bridleway signpost points left, but there is scarcely a trodden path. Just beforehand, however, a clear track, well marked by stone uprights, heads up to the left, crossing the moorland crest. Follow this, looking ahead for the highest building in view on the other side. Keep to the left of the farmhouse to join its access track and walk down to a nearby minor road. Keep right to follow the road across a **cattle-grid**, then later turn left as signposted for Lealholm near **Wind Hill**. The road drops steeply and bends left, and there is also a short climb uphill to a junction. Turn right downhill and cross the bridge over the **River Esk** to return to the village of **Lealholm**, and either take a break there or walk back up the path to the railway station.

WALK 35
Glaisdale Rigg, Egton High Moor and Egton Bridge

Distance	21km (13 miles)
Start/finish	Glaisdale Railway Station, Eskdale, GR 783055
Maps	OS Landranger 94; OS Explorer OL27 North
Terrain	A long tough walk where quiet roads and clear tracks are used at first; the path used to descend into Glaisdale needs care and is rather vague; other moorland paths are clear, but the high moors are exposed
Refreshments	Arncliffe Arms and Mitre Tavern at Glaisdale, Horseshoe Hotel at Egton Bridge
Transport	Arriva trains serve Glaisdale and Egton Bridge from Whitby and Middlesbrough

There are high moorland roads alongside and around the head of Glaisdale, so a high-level circuit might be better made on a bicycle than on foot. Walkers would prefer to climb alongside Glaisdale, then drop down into the head of the dale and climb up the other side to appreciate its quiet charms. To avoid the road on the other side of the dale, it is better to follow a clear and obvious path across Egton High Moor, and eventually descend to Egton Bridge. There are railway stations at Glaisdale and Egton Bridge, but there is also an opportunity to link both places using a road and a footpath.

Leave **Glaisdale Railway Station**, where there are toilets, and turn right up the road to the Arncliffe Arms, which offers food, drink and accommodation. Turn right downhill to follow the road near the river, then climb steeply up to the Mitre Tavern in **Glaisdale** village. Turn right to walk up High Terrace through the rest of the village, passing the village shop. Turn left at the top of the road, at a triangular green, to go up **Hall Lane**. The tarmac expires at a gate and a stony track leads out onto heathery **Glaisdale Moor**. Simply follow the broad clear track uphill, avoiding other tracks and paths to either side, and cross a dip on the moorland slopes.

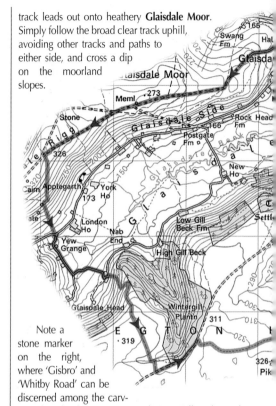

Note a stone marker on the right, where 'Gisbro' and 'Whitby Road' can be discerned among the carvings, though other names are indistinct. Follow the track up **Glaisdale Rigg** to the top at 326m (1070ft), but stop just short of a tarmac road. Turn left along and down a track, which gradually becomes a vague path and eventually vanishes among bilberry and bracken. Don't be in too much of a hurry to drop down into Glaisdale, but drift to the right and maybe head for a drystone wall, then turn left downhill on a short steep bracken slope at **Red House**. (There is no house here, only a tin hut nearby.) Go through a little gate and walk down through fields and another couple of small gates to reach a road junction.

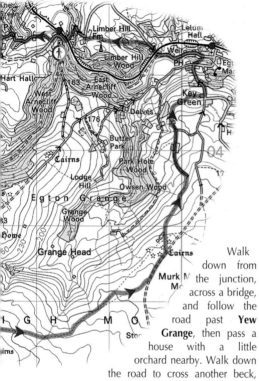

Walk down from the junction, across a bridge, and follow the road past **Yew Grange**, then pass a house with a little orchard nearby. Walk down the road to cross another beck, then up the road and round the back of some houses. Turn right as signposted public bridleway, up a rough-pasture field and through a gate. Bend right and left, passing close to a forest, then away from the forest and up a moorland slope to a gate. Follow a rugged path over a heather moor, which becomes easier and passes a stone-walled enclosure in a gentle dip. Follow a track up to a road, then turn left to follow the road alongside a forest at **Wintergill Plantation**.

Turn right to leave the road along a moorland track signposted as a public footpath. The track runs almost level at 320m (1050ft) over heathery **Egton High Moor**. There is

Walkers follow the long track up Glaisdale Rigg to reach the higher moors

a view of a pond off to the right, but keep following the clear track, which runs gently downhill over heather and bilberry to pass a lonesome pine tree. Note how the track appears to head for a portion of the sea around Whitby, but suddenly swings right to land on a minor road on **Murk Mire Moor**. Turn left to follow the road, passing a public footpath signpost as well as a prominent stone upright.

Turn left at a public bridleway signpost and follow a path through a groove in the heather and bracken moor. Cross a path, then walk down a rather wet and boggy path, through bracken, to reach a **pair of gates** marked with blue arrows. Walk straight ahead, following a vague path across a rough pasture. Go through another gate and keep straight ahead, then later a grassy track swings left downhill. Follow it through the farmyard at **Swang Farm**, then follow the access track downhill away from the farm.

When the access track turns right uphill, turn left to leave it and follow a short grassy track flanked by trees to reach a gate. Walk past the left-hand side of a barn as signposted along a footpath, and continue along a grassy path flanked by trees and bushes, including plenty of holly. The path becomes a clear track that leads to a road at **Key Green**. Turn left down the road where the Horseshoe Hotel at the bottom offers food, drink and accommodation. There are two sets of stepping stones across the **River Esk** between the hotel and the village of **Egton Bridge**, but if the river is flowing too high, follow the road round to the village, crossing a nearby bridge. There are toilets in the village, as well as a railway station if you wish to cut the route short and save walking the last 2.5km (1.5 miles).

To continue with the walk, leave **Egton Bridge** by road, walking upstream alongside the **River Esk**, where a placid stretch of the river is held behind a weir. The road later veers away from the river and climbs uphill, under a railway arch, passing **Broom House** bed and breakfast. Watch for a step-stile on the left, then walk along a woodland fence leading uphill. Cross a dip and walk up to a stile to enter a stand of conifers, then climb further uphill. Exit from the trees and walk alongside a field, then cross a stile and continue straight along a track. Keep to the left of all the buildings at **Limber Hill Farm**, where the track can be muddy. Turn right to reach a road bend, then turn left to walk down the road. To avoid the lower part of the road, turn left over a step-stile as signposted public footpath. Cross a field and go down a steep and narrow woodland path. This leads straight onto the slender stone arch of **Beggar's Bridge**. Cross over and follow the road under a railway arch, then simply turn right to finish back at **Glaisdale Railway Station**.

Black clouds pile up in the sky over bleak and barren Egton High Moor

THE EASTERN MOORS

Many would claim that the Eastern Moors are part of the High Moors, but there is a distinct change in the moorlands as walkers progress eastwards. They dwindle in height, and although they still look broad, bleak and barren, forestry and cultivation have made great inroads into them. The peculiar pyramidal radar site at RAF Fylingdales is an abiding feature in this part of the North York Moors – a structure as incongruous as the monstrous 'golf ball' radomes that preceded it.

Drawing a line between the High Moors and the Eastern Moors could be done in a number of ways. The deep-cleft gorge of Newtondale, through which the North Yorkshire Moors Railway runs, is an obvious choice, the busy main A169 is another, but for the purposes of this guidebook the dividing line is Wheeldale. You could regard the low sprawling moorland of Simon Howe as part of the High Moors, but its character fits more into the Eastern Moors mould, and as it is traversed from Goathland, it has something further in common with other walks in this section of the guidebook.

Goathland is well known to those who follow the popular 'Heartbeat' TV series, and out of the six walks in this area, four are centred on that lovely village. Goathland is the starting point for a walk over Simon Howe, returning through Wheeldale. The Historic Rail Trail passes through the village on its way to Grosmont, where walkers can keep the theme in full steam by enjoying a ride on the North Yorkshire Moors Railway. Two more walks head eastwards onto the broad moorland slopes, one climbing uphill to take a close look at a curious geological feature known as Whinstone Ridge, and the other running high along the crest of Lilla Howe. The moorlands around Lilla Howe are so extensive that another walk is described tackling the slopes from Harwood Dale. The final offering in this section is a varied valley walk from Sleights.

There is actually one further walk in this area, and that is the last route in this guidebook, where the Lyke Wake Walk takes an astonishingly direct line across the moors to finish high above the coast at Ravenscar.

WALK 36
Goathland, Simon Howe, Wheeldale and Mallyan Spout

Distance	15km (9.5 miles)
Start/finish	Mallyan Spout Hotel, Goathland, GR 827007
Maps	OS Landranger 94; OS Explorers OL27 South and OL27 North
Terrain	A moderate walk along good moorland tracks and paths, with one vague stretch, then forest tracks are followed; fiddly field paths give way to an awkward, bouldery, muddy walk along a wooded riverside path
Refreshments	Mallyan Spout Hotel and other places down the road in Goathland
Transport	Yorkshire Coastliner buses serve Goathland from Whitby and Pickering; North Yorkshire Moors Railway serves Goathland from Grosmont and Pickering

Simon Howe is a broad moorland, but not particularly high or extensive. However, it does stand somewhat in isolation, rising between Wheeldale and Newtondale, and offering extensive views around Fylingdales Moor and the high moors. An ascent is easily accomplished from Goathland, then moorland paths and forest tracks can be used to link with the ancient 'Roman' road at Wheeldale. A rather awkward, bouldery, muddy and slippery walk alongside West Beck leads to the delicate waterfall of Mallyan Spout, from where a return to Goathland is made up a long flight of steps.

Start at the top end of **Goathland** village, beside the church and **Mallyan Spout Hotel**. Walk along the road signposted for Egton Bridge, but only until the Jubilee Tree and **Pinfold** is seen on the left. Fork left up a grassy path signposted as a public bridleway. There are a couple of paths branching up to the left, but you must

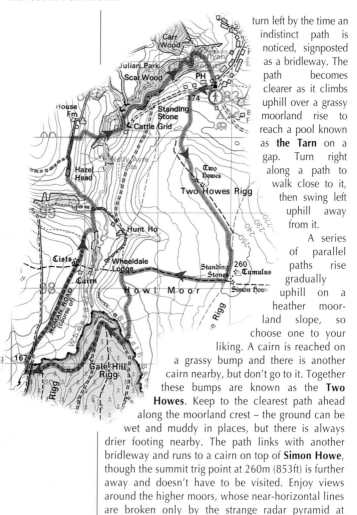

turn left by the time an indistinct path is noticed, signposted as a bridleway. The path becomes clearer as it climbs uphill over a grassy moorland rise to reach a pool known as **the Tarn** on a gap. Turn right along a path to walk close to it, then swing left uphill away from it.

A series of parallel paths rise gradually uphill on a heather moorland slope, so choose one to your liking. A cairn is reached on a grassy bump and there is another cairn nearby, but don't go to it. Together these bumps are known as the **Two Howes**. Keep to the clearest path ahead along the moorland crest – the ground can be wet and muddy in places, but there is always drier footing nearby. The path links with another bridleway and runs to a cairn on top of **Simon Howe**, though the summit trig point at 260m (853ft) is further away and doesn't have to be visited. Enjoy views around the higher moors, whose near-horizontal lines are broken only by the strange radar pyramid at RAF Fylingdales.

Turn right to follow a clear path heading westwards away from **Simon Howe**. The path on the

heather moor can be wet and muddy in places, then a firm, dry gritstone edge is reached overlooking **Wheeldale Lodge**, formerly a youth hostel. (An obvious short cut across Wheeldale is possible here.)

Walkers follow the rough and stony course of the Wheeldale 'Roman' Road

Turn left at a signpost to follow a clear path, and keep to the clearest path at junctions with other paths on the heather moor. Look ahead to spot another signpost later, but bear in mind that the path becomes quite vague before it reaches a small footbridge over **Blawath Beck** near a forest. Walk up to a forest track and turn right, then keep right at junctions with all other tracks around **Gale Hill Rigg** so that the main track leads to a gate and out of the forest. Turn right down a road to reach a footbridge and ford on **Wheeldale Beck** then follow the road uphill. Branch right to cross a stile beside an information board and follow **Wheeldale Road**.

WHEELDALE ROAD

Ancient Wheeldale Road is also known as Wade's Causeway. A giant by the name of Wade is said to have built the road for his wife Bell to herd her sheep along. For a long time it was assumed to be a Roman road, though some archaeologists now doubt this and suggest that it may be late Roman or even pre-Roman.

Follow the old road across the moor, perhaps walking alongside as the surface is rather rough and bouldery. Pass a gate and ladder stile to follow an even rougher stretch downhill. When another **information board** is reached, drift right and left, as marked, down through fields and continue down a clear track. Use a gate and stile on the right, then cross a footbridge over **Wheeldale Gill** near a ford. Turn left to follow a path, screened by trees, straight uphill from the ford. Bear right on the way up, and go through a gate and along a hollow way to pass in front of **Hazel Head farm**. Follow the access road away from the farm, going through gates, then watch for a public bridleway signpost beside a small gate on the right. Turn right and walk downhill to go through another small gate, then turn left. Turn right at the next gate, then left at the bottom of a field to follow a woodland path downhill. Go through a tiny meadow and pass a house, then cross a long footbridge over **West**

Mallyan Spout is a delicate curtain-like waterfall not far from Goathland

Beck. Walk up to a concrete access road and turn right up to a minor road. Turn left down the road, then turn right at a bridge to follow a path.

Be warned that the riverside path is rough and bouldery, and there are slippery tree roots exposed in places. When the path becomes wet and muddy it needs even more care. The rugged wooded valley through which **West Beck** flows is like a jungle in places. Two footbridges are crossed before wooden steps lead up to **Mallyan Spout**, which is a delicate, feathery curtain of water spilling down a mossy face. Continue along the riverside path, heading downstream to a prominent path junction. The path continuing downstream to Beck Hole is very pleasant, but turn right instead up a long flight of steps to return to the **Mallyan Spout Hotel**.

WALK 37
Rail Trail from Moorgates to Goathland and Grosmont

Distance	8km (5 miles)
Start	Moorgates, near Goathland, GR 844994
Finish	Grosmont Railway Station, GR 828052
Maps	OS Landranger 94; OS Explorer OL27 North
Terrain	Easy walk along level, firm dry tracks in a valley and woodlands
Refreshments	Snack van at Abbot's House Farm, pubs and restaurants at Goathland and Grosmont
Transport	Yorkshire Coastliner buses pass Moorgates and Goathland, North Yorkshire Moors Railway serves Goathland and Grosmont from Pickering, and Arriva trains link Grosmont with Whitby and Middlesbrough

The North Yorkshire Moors Railway is a well-known attraction, with steam trains running between Pickering, Levisham, Goathland and Grosmont. The line from Pickering to Whitby was constructed by George Stephenson and opened in 1836, the first passengers travelling in horse-drawn carriages because steam trains were unable to use a 1:5 incline at Beck Hole. When George Hudson bought the line he diverted the track from Beck Hole in 1865 so that steam engines could use the line. However, a branch line to Beck Hole was maintained so that summer services from Whitby operated even as late as 1914. The old trackbed now offers a short and easy low-level linear Rail Trail.

As this route is linear you should use the Yorkshire Coastliner bus to reach **Moorgates**, between Goathland and the main A169 at Eller Beck. This was once a level crossing and the road passes arches on both the current and former railway lines. Start at the old house beside the

The old railway trackbed to Goathland is joined at Moor Crossing at Moorgates

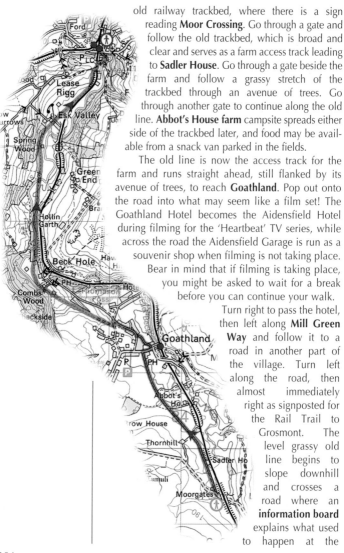

old railway trackbed, where there is a sign reading **Moor Crossing**. Go through a gate and follow the old trackbed, which is broad and clear and serves as a farm access track leading to **Sadler House**. Go through a gate beside the farm and follow a grassy stretch of the trackbed through an avenue of trees. Go through another gate to continue along the old line. **Abbot's House farm** campsite spreads either side of the trackbed later, and food may be available from a snack van parked in the fields.

The old line is now the access track for the farm and runs straight ahead, still flanked by its avenue of trees, to reach **Goathland**. Pop out onto the road into what may seem like a film set! The Goathland Hotel becomes the Aidensfield Hotel during filming for the 'Heartbeat' TV series, while across the road the Aidensfield Garage is run as a souvenir shop when filming is not taking place. Bear in mind that if filming is taking place, you might be asked to wait for a break before you can continue your walk.

Turn right to pass the hotel, then left along **Mill Green Way** and follow it to a road in another part of the village. Turn left along the road, then almost immediately right as signposted for the Rail Trail to Grosmont. The level grassy old line begins to slope downhill and crosses a road where an **information board** explains what used to happen at the incline at this point. The line was a twin track, and while carriages were lowered up and down one line, heavy water barrels were hauled up and down the other to counterbalance them. Walk down the old trackbed into the dense woodlands of a valley. The trees thin out at a gateway and the route continues past **Incline Cottage** where the old line levels out. Cross a footbridge and pass the site of **Beck Hole Station**.

The trackbed continues, sometimes with views on either side and sometimes through woodlands that obscure views. Cross two footbridges mounted on the original supports that carried the old railway across the **Murk Esk**. After following the line through fields with more open views, cross another footbridge mounted on the old bridge abutments, then the line runs mostly through woods. Pass a **stone house** and continue through a small wooded cutting. Pass between a row of houses and a converted chapel, then the trackbed is quite broad and cindery, and gradually runs close to the current railway line. Look along the line to see the **engine sheds** on the North York Moors Railway, although there is no access to them from this side.

Follow a gravel path uphill and go through a gate. Turn right, crossing high above a tunnel that carries the railway, then turn left through a gate and follow a broad, stony woodland path downhill alongside St Matthew's Church. The village of **Grosmont** is directly ahead, but you might first consider turning left to follow a path straight through a tunnel to see the **engine sheds**. The tunnel was cut between 1833 and 1835 under the direction of George Stephenson and is thought to be the world's first railway tunnel. The walk finishes at **Grosmont Railway Station** and you should note that there are actually two stations side by side. One is operated by the North York Moors Railway, and the other by Arriva, connecting with Whitby and Middlesbrough.

WALK 38
Goathland, Sleights Moor and Whinstone Ridge

Distance	6.5km (4 miles)
Start/finish	Goathland Railway Station, GR 836013
Maps	OS Landranger 94; OS Explorer OL27 North
Terrain	A moderate short walk where moorland paths vary from good to untrodden, while low-level paths and tracks are clear throughout
Refreshments	Goathland Hotel and other places up the road in Goathland
Transport	Yorkshire Coastliner buses serve Goathland from Whitby and Pickering, North Yorkshire Moors Railway serves Goathland from Grosmont and Pickering

Across Goathland Moor and beyond, a linear feature called Whinstone Ridge is marked on maps, but there is no ridge. Walkers will find a deep trough cut into the moorland and piles of rubble being colonised by vegetation. There *was* once a ridge – a hard upstanding dyke of basalt, also known as the Cleveland Dyke, squeezed in a molten state into surrounding bedrock almost 60 million years ago. It was quarried away for roadstone, being highly prized in an area that generally features only crumbling sandstone, shale and limestone. Climb high above Goathland to see this awesome gash on the moors, then drop down to Darnholme on the way back to Goathland.

Start from **Goathland Railway Station** and climb a path straight up from the station platform, on the opposite side of the track to Goathland village. When a junction is reached only a short way uphill, turn right along a level grassy path, then turn left up a narrow grassy path on a slope of bracken. The vegetation changes to heather as height is gained, then the path expires at a square-cut pool on the moorland, which is an old **reservoir**. The higher parts of the moorland slope are untrodden, but head straight uphill on a course that gradually converges with a road, and the road should be reached at a point where a public footpath signpost points back along your invisible route. Turn left to continue walking up the road, and use the verges for safety's sake if there is any amount of traffic. Walk as far as a **road junction** and turn left, as signposted for Green End and Beck Hole.

Immediately after turning left, step off the road to the right and follow a path through a deep groove scored down the moorland slope. This was where **Whinstone Ridge** ran before it was quarried away. Walk in the bottom of the cut, though later it might be better to keep to the moorland on one side or the other if the floor of the cut gets too rough and stony. Keep following the quarried entrenchment over **Sleights Moor** until enclosures are reached around high fields. Turn left along a gravel track to return to the road. Cross over the road to continue as signposted along a public footpath.

Follow a clear and grassy path down a slope of heather. Keep left down a track, then keep left again at a gate, following a path that steepens as it drops into a valley. Go down a partially wooded slope and cross a **footbridge** at the bottom to reach a track. Turn right along the track to reach a ford at **Darnholme**, but there is no need to cross over. Simply turn left to walk a short way upstream beside **Eller Beck**, then turn left again up a steep flight of stone steps above the railway line. Continue alongside a drystone wall, across a moorland slope, until a path that was used earlier in the day drops down to the right and leads straight back onto the platform at **Goathland Railway Station**.

187

Darnholme is a pleasant little huddle of houses seen beside Eller Beck

WALK 39
Goathland, Eller Beck, Lilla Howe and Goathland Moor

Distance	17km (10.5 miles)
Start/finish	Goathland Railway Station, GR 836013
Maps	OS Landranger 94; OS Explorers OL27 North and South
Terrain	A tough walk, starting with a clear track and road followed by clear moorland paths and tracks; a road and vague path are used on the descent, and the high moors are exposed
Refreshments	Goathland Hotel at Goathland, snack van at Abbot's House Farm
Transport	Yorkshire Coastliner buses serve Goathland from Whitby and Pickering, and North Yorkshire Moors Railway serves Goathland from Grosmont and Pickering

Here's a route that starts in gentle pastures around Goathland and climbs onto bleak and barren Goathland Moor and Fylingdales Moor. Apart from the dominance of RAF Fylingdales and its strange central pyramid, walkers will spot a handful of stone uprights that have been planted along the crest of the moorland over the centuries. Lilla Cross is undoubtedly one of the most striking moorland markers, but the less well-known examples are just as interesting in their own right. The busy A169 is an intrusion into the wilds, but it bisects this route and care is needed when crossing or following it.

Start from **Goathland Railway Station** and walk up into the village to reach the Goathland Hotel, which sometimes becomes the Aidensfield Hotel when filming is in progress for the 'Heartbeat' TV series. Turn left beside the hotel along a clear track signposted as a public bridleway. The track is flanked by an avenue of trees and runs to the **Abbot's House farm** campsite, where food might be available from a snack van. Keep straight ahead along the track, which is the trackbed of an old

189

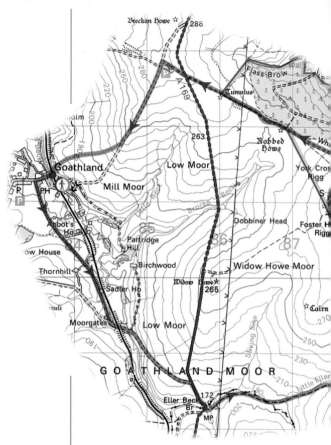

railway, and go through a gate to follow a grassy stretch. Go through another gate beside **Sadler House** and continue to reach a road at **Moorgates**. Turn left and walk down the road, going under a railway arch and crossing **Eller Beck**. Follow the road uphill to join the busy **A169**, and turn right to follow this road, walking with care along the right-hand side, facing the traffic, to cross **Eller Beck Bridge**.

Turn left to leave the road and follow a track that is clearly marked as running onto **MOD property** – part of RAF Fylingdales. Cross a stile beside a gate and walk beneath a pylon line to the end of the track. Keep to the left-hand side of a fence to continue, following a path across a boggy area full of bog myrtle. The path aligns itself to **Little Eller Beck** and pulls away from the fence. There is a line of white posts planted all the way up the heather moorland slope, and the path is always well to the left of them. It can be muddy underfoot in places, but later a firm gravel track is reached and a left turn leads to a gate. Go through the gate and cross another track, walking straight ahead up a more rugged path on a heather slope. Cross a rough track then aim for **Lilla Cross** on Lilla Howe, at 292m (958ft). Although of no great height, this moorland top offers extensive views through the heart of the North York Moors.

Walk back a short way downhill and turn right along the rugged track to reach a signposted intersection of tracks – directions given include 'Robin Hood's Bay', 'Harwood Dale', 'Saltergate' and 'Goathland'. Take the last one, which is a matter of turning left and walking gently uphill to **Louven Howe**. A heathery mound is crowned with a stone stump and a trig point at 299m (981ft). Continue

LILLA CROSS

Of all the crosses dotted around the North York Moors National Park, Lilla Cross is reckoned to be the oldest. It stands on a Bronze Age burial mound and was erected to commemorate Lilla, a minister to King Edwin of Northumbria whose intervention during an assassination attempt on the king led to his own death in 626 AD. The cross was removed for safe keeping when the moors were used for military training, then later replanted.

Eller Beck Bridge is crossed close to MOD property at RAF Fylingdales

along the track and cross over another broader track to go straight ahead through a gate. Walk gently along and down a rugged moorland track along a broad heathery crest. There is always a fence to the right, then the track climbs very gently uphill, passing **Ann's Cross** on a tumulus. Keep walking along the track and go through a gate where the twin heathery humps of **Foster Howes** are off to the left.

The track continues and the fence is now on the left-hand side. However, the track swings right, away from the fence, then left, running gradually downhill to level out beside a forest. The track is actually following the course of **Whinstone Ridge**, a dyke of igneous rock intruded into the bedrock of the moors. Pass the heathery hump of **Robbed Howe** and climb gently uphill beneath a pylon line, also passing a bridleway signpost where a tumulus on the right is topped with a couple of stone uprights. Continue gently uphill to reach the busy **A169** at a lay-by. Cross the road with care and go through a gate to continue along a short grassy track, over a heathery rise, to reach a quieter road on **Sleights Moor**.

Turn left to walk down the road, on the right-hand side, and watch out for a public footpath signpost pointing down to the right. There is no sign of a trodden path on the moorland slope, and some walkers might prefer to stay on the road. However, by walking straight down towards a square-cut pool, which turns out to be an old **reservoir**, a good path will be found leading further downhill through heather and bracken. When a better path is reached, turn right along it for a short way, then turn left to drop straight downhill to land back on the platform at **Goathland Railway Station**.

WALK 40
Chapel Farm, Lilla Howe and Jugger Howe Beck

Distance	17km (10.5 miles)
Start/finish	Chapel Farm, GR 952967
Maps	OS Landranger 94 or 101; OS Explorer OL27 South
Terrain	A tough walk where rugged woodland paths quickly give way to clear farm tracks and moorland tracks; paths through the valley towards the end are quite rugged too
Refreshments	Grainary Hotel off-route in Harwood Dale
Transport	None to Chapel Farm, though regular Arriva buses run along the nearby A171 at Helwath Bridge, between Whitby and Scarborough

Here is a route around a quiet part of Fylingdales Moor, access being from Chapel Farm on the Helwath road in Harwood Dale. The route passes through Castlebeck Wood and climbs gradually through huge fields that have been wrested from the moorland slopes. A fine clear track can be followed onto the higher moors, even to the extent of visiting Lilla Cross on Lilla Howe. The return route wanders gently down another moorland track, passing Burn Howe and leading into the rugged valley drained by Jugger Howe Beck. The beck leads back into the wooded valley below Chapel Farm.

Start at **Chapel Farm** in Harwood Dale, where a signpost beside the road reads 'Bridleway to Lilla'. The path descends through nettles, then runs down a field, turning right through a gate where the Woodland Trust welcomes walkers to **Castlebeck Wood**. Walk down into the woods and cross a footbridge over **Jugger Howe Beck**. Walk uphill and swing left up a muddy groove to reach a small gate at the top of the wooded slope. Turn right through fields to reach a building at **Park Hill**, and keep to the left

193

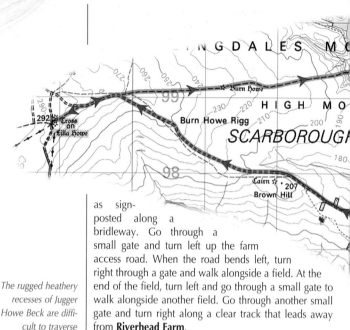

The rugged heathery recesses of Jugger Howe Beck are difficult to traverse

as sign-posted along a bridleway. Go through a small gate and turn left up the farm access road. When the road bends left, turn right through a gate and walk alongside a field. At the end of the field, turn left and go through a small gate to walk alongside another field. Go through another small gate and turn right along a clear track that leads away from **Riverhead Farm**.

194

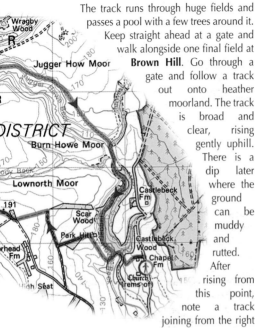

The track runs through huge fields and passes a pool with a few trees around it. Keep straight ahead at a gate and walk alongside one final field at **Brown Hill**. Go through a gate and follow a track out onto heather moorland. The track is broad and clear, rising gently uphill. There is a dip later where the ground can be muddy and rutted. After rising from this point, note a track joining from the right at a boulder, as you will return here later. For now, keep straight ahead up the track, then branch left up a lesser path to reach the prominent **Lilla Cross** on Lilla Howe. This stands at 292m (958ft), and though of no great height, there are extensive views through the heart of the North York Moors.

Walk back down the path from Lilla Howe, keeping right along a track to return to the junction where the boulder noted earlier is. Branch left along a track that can be rough and stony as well as muddy when wet. It is clear and obvious at it descends gently over **Fylingdales Moor**, passing a cairn on a mound known as **Burn Howe**. The track becomes a narrow path, but remains clear to follow, then becomes quite rugged before steepening as it drops towards **Jugger Howe Beck**. Cross the wet and muddy land near the beck and cross the beck too. Start

195

Lilla Cross may be the oldest of all the moorland crosses in the North York Moors

following a path uphill, but watch for a marker pointing right and follow a lesser path in that direction.

Keep looking ahead to try and spot the line of this path, which is rather vague as it forges along the rugged valley side. It heads downstream roughly parallel to Jugger Howe Beck, but often quite some distance away from the stream. Bracken, heather and bog myrtle slopes are traversed, and eventually the path reaches a footbridge over **Helwath Beck**. Cross over and keep right to walk downstream alongside Jugger Howe Beck again. Cross another footbridge and turn left to continue along a woodland path. This eventually leads back to the first footbridge that was crossed at the start of the day. Simply cross over the beck one last time and follow the path back up to the road at **Chapel Farm**.

WALK 41
Sleights, Ugglebarnby, Falling Foss and Littlebeck

Distance	13km (8 miles)
Start/finish	Sleights Railway Station, GR 868081
Maps	OS Landranger 94; OS Explorer OL27 North
Terrain	A moderate walk along a fairly fiddly selection of paths and tracks that run through fields, alongside moorland, through woods, more fields and along riversides
Refreshments	Plough Inn and Salmon Leap in Sleights
Transport	Arriva trains, Arriva buses and Yorkshire Coastliner buses serve Sleights from Whitby

This is essentially a valley walk, though it does climb high above Sleights and reaches the fringes of Ugglebarnby Moor. After dropping back down into a wooded valley, the route includes a glimpse of Falling Foss, which is a gentle, slender waterfall most of the time. The woods between the waterfall and Littlebeck are managed as a nature reserve. Various paths are linked together to form a route that runs roughly parallel to Little Beck on the way back to Sleights. The route is structured from the railway station, but it could be covered just as easily from bus services in the village.

Start from **Sleights Railway Station** and walk along Lowdale Lane, which later runs beside **Little Beck**. Turn right up a road, then left at Whin Green, which is signposted as a public footpath. At the end of the tarmac, cross a narrow footbridge on the left and let a paved and grassy path lead to a house. Keep to the left of the main buildings as marked then drift right uphill. Watch out on the right for a **footbridge** and cross it, then climb steeply to locate a path on a wooded slope. Follow this, then walk alongside a field and cross a couple of stiles to reach a road. Turn left up the road towards the village of **Ugglebarnby**, but just before reaching a road junction turn right along jungly, overgrown **Tom Bell Lane**. Stretches of a flagstone causeway are seen along the way from time to time, but some parts are rather muddy. Eventually turn left up a broader track and continue up past the buildings at **Dean Hall** to reach a minor road.

Turn right down the road, then branch left as signposted along a public bridleway, before **Hempsyke Hall**, to follow a path into woods. Keep straight ahead until forced to turn left uphill by a wall. Continue through woods and out onto a heather moorland dotted with conifers. Keep to the path alongside **Ugglebarnby Moor** and reach a farm. Follow the access track away, but watch out on the right for a bridleway signpost and arrow indicating a path through woods and bracken to a nearby minor road. Cross the road and continue along a signposted footpath. This runs through bracken, with views of the moor, then crosses a farm access track near **Thorn Hill**. The path is lightly trodden, though clear enough, with more views of the moor and its scrub woodland. Reach a house and turn right down a minor road.

The road runs down into the woods of **Falling Foss Forest Nature Reserve**. Walk to the right, down a gravel track dropping steeply from a car park, and branch right to continue down a gravel path to find a viewpoint for the waterfall of **Falling Foss**. Keep to the right to follow the clearest path up and across the wooded valley sides, reaching a path junction where a left turn is signposted for Littlebeck. Turn left and follow the path down to **the Hermitage**, a rock outcrop with a shelter carved into it. Continue straight ahead and down stone steps, crossing muddy patches, slippery tree roots and boulders, into **Little Beck Wood**, which is managed as a nature reserve by the Yorkshire Wildlife Trust. Some stretches of the path feature duckboards, then the path climbs up, around and down a crumbling hump of shale with a cave cut into its base. Exit from the wood and turn right, steeply uphill along a minor road in the small settlement of **Littlebeck**.

Pass Littlebeck village hall and car park, then take the road signposted for Whitby, which climbs uphill. Turn left as signposted along a public footpath, through a gate and down a grassy track. Continue across the top side of some fields, then along the bottom side of a field above **Low Farm**. Turn left to go down past the farm, then right to walk downstream alongside **Little Beck**. Use a good track and path, then cross some stepping stones over the beck near **Throstle Nest** before using a footbridge to cross back again. Climb a ladder stile and continue through fields, and later cross a step-stile to follow a short, wooded riverside path. The rest of the path is enclosed and eventually reaches **Mill Lane** and some cottages at **Iburndale**.

Turn left along a road to cross a bridge, then right to follow a short track between houses. This narrows to a squeeze-path, which soon broadens and runs alongside **Little Beck**. When you finally reach tarmac you are following your earliest footsteps of the day, so simply turn right and left by road to walk back to **Sleights Railway Station** to complete the walk.

THE CLEVELAND COAST

By the time the North York Moors National Park reaches the coast the moorlands have already given way to gentle cultivated countryside cleft by wooded valleys. Whitby, at the point where the River Esk spills into the North Sea, is the only place of any size, a former whaling town that has turned its hand to tourism. There are several villages too, including lovely Staithes, Runswick Bay, Kettleness, Sandsend, Robin Hood's Bay and the peculiar 'failed resort' of Ravenscar. Between each settlement there are fine cliffs, and because of the Jurassic geology, wealth of fossils, abundant wildlife and abiding historical interest of these dramatic cliffs, the whole coastline has been designated the Cleveland Heritage Coast. A peculiar weather feature along the coast is the dense fog, or 'roak', that sometimes blows in from the sea.

After leaving the moors the Cleveland Way enjoys a splendid romp along cliff paths all the way from Saltburn-on-Sea to Scarborough and Filey, even including cliffs that lie outside the national park boundary to get the most from the coast. Many visitors who enjoy good walks are familiar with the cliff coast, but not all of them realise that there is another walking route available a short way inland, running roughly parallel to the coast. There was once a coastal railway linking Scarborough with Whitby and Saltburn, beyond, but only the northern stretch survives as a mineral line. The whole of the rest of the line between Scarborough and Whitby has been retained as a Rail Trail walkway and cycleway, tying in with the coast path at various settlements along the way.

Five walks are described along the coast, and four of these make use of stretches of the old railway line (which operated from 1885 to 1965) so that a series of fine circular walks can be completed. On the first walk the old line is barely noticed between Runswick Bay and Staithes, and the cliff coast path is used to link both charming villages. Another stretch of coastal path links Runswick Bay with Kettleness, returning along the old railway trackbed. The cliff coast walk from Whitby to Robin Hood's Bay is a short classic walk, and the old line used further inland is plain and obvious throughout. Similarly, the short coast walk from Robin Hood's Bay to Ravenscar returns along the line. Finally, a longer stretch of the old trackbed is followed from Cloughton to Ravenscar, returning along the roller-coaster cliff path afterwards. Together these routes allow most of the Cleveland Coast to be explored, along with most of the Rail Trail further inland. Strong walkers can of course combine any two walks that share a common link and extend each day's explorations.

WALK 42
Runswick Bay, Hinderwell, Staithes and Port Mulgrave

Distance	11.5km (7 miles)
Start/finish	Runswick Bay Hotel, GR 806161
Maps	OS Landranger 94; OS Explorer OL27 North
Terrain	Easy walking along clear roads, tracks and paths leading inland, with a couple of vague stretches; a clear cliff coast path closes the circuit
Refreshments	Pubs at Hinderwell, pubs at Dalehouse and Port Mulgrave, pubs, restaurants and cafés at Staithes and Runswick Bay
Transport	Regular Arriva buses link Runswick Bay, Hinderwell and Staithes with Whitby, Guisborough and Middlesbrough

The coastal walk between the lovely little harbour at Staithes and the amazing stack of houses at Runswick Bay is fairly popular, but few walkers venture inland, where an interesting wooded valley called the Dales is located. This walk starts at Runswick Bay and heads inland first, bypassing Hinderwell to go down through the Dales, then climbs over to Staithes to explore the crooked little harbour and its associations with the young James Cook. Afterwards a fine cliff coast walk leads to Port Mulgrave, an old ironstone port which was actually serviced by tunnels from Grinkle, far inland. Another fine stretch of cliff coast returns walkers to Runswick Bay.

Start at the **Runswick Bay Hotel** and follow Hinderwell Lane, which is signposted for Hinderwell and has a pavement alongside throughout its length. When the first houses are reached at **Hinderwell**, turn left as signposted along a public footpath and walk alongside a field to reach the main A174. Turn right along the road, then take the first turning on the left along **Brown's Terrace**. Walk off the end of the tarmac road to follow a track known as

Hinderwell Back Lane. Turn right and the track becomes grassy, then later turn right again and it becomes an earth track studded with bricks and masonry. There are bushy hedgerows that allow only occasional glimpses of Hinderwell village.

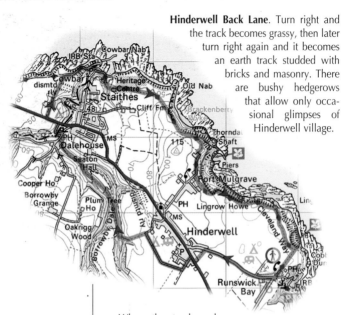

When the track makes another turn to the right, turn left instead to walk downhill alongside a field. Continue straight down a grassy slope and straight down again into the wooded valley known as **the Dales**. Cross a footbridge over a beck and climb up steps on the other side, then go through a small gate to leave the wood at the top of the slope and turn right alongside a field. Cross a stile back into the wood and turn left, following a narrow path through dense woodland planted along a ridge beside **Borrowby Dale**. Watch for a yellow sign just to the left, reading 'Oakridge Nature Reserve', and pass it. A clear path reaches a gate and you continue along a broad grassy swathe surrounded by woodland. Walk down a steep gravel path to a small **caravan site** and follow the access track away across a bridge. Walk down a concrete road to reach a bridge at **Dalehouse** and turn right along a road to reach the Fox and Hounds pub.

Turn left beside the pub to cross a narrow bridge where an old road has been blocked against traffic and become rather overgrown. Follow it uphill by swinging right, then cross the main **A174** with care. Turn left and walk on the right-hand side of the road, facing oncoming traffic for safety, while crossing a rise. Turn right along the access road for **Cowbar farm**, and keep right of the farm to follow a path under an old stone railway arch in the fields beyond. Walk straight across a field to reach a minor road and turn right to follow the road down to the charming, colourful village of **Staithes**. Cross the footbridge over the narrow harbour to reach the main part of the village.

The narrow and attractive harbour and higgledy-piggledy houses at Staithes

STAITHES

The narrow natural harbour, with its protective projecting cliff face at Cowbar Nab, made Staithes an ideal retreat for fishermen, traders and smugglers. Latterly the higgledy-piggledy houses and narrow alleys have enchanted artists and photographers. For a thorough grounding in the history of this delightfully jumbled village, be sure to visit the Captain Cook & Staithes Heritage Centre. The teenage James Cook worked as an assistant to a Staithes shopkeeper called William Sanderson. The sea destroyed the original shop, but parts of it were incorporated into Captain Cook's Cottage. Cook stayed for only 18 months, then moved to Whitby to train as an apprentice seaman and embark on his seafaring career.

After crossing the footbridge over the harbour at **Staithes**, walk up to a narrow cobbled street and turn left to reach **the Cod & Lobster**, which has been partially demolished by storms on three occasions. Turn right up Church Street and pass **Captain Cook's Cottage**. Follow the stone-paved Cleveland Way even further uphill to leave the village, taking a last fond look back at the intriguing jumble of cottages.

Turn left, as signposted for Runswick Bay, and follow a clear path past a farm. Walk through fields and climb a steep grassy slope to regain the cliff path. Keep climbing uphill, almost to 100m (330ft) on **Beacon Hill**. The next road, Rosedale Lane, could be followed inland from **Port Mulgrave** to reach the Ship Inn for food and drink, otherwise stay on the route.

PORT MULGRAVE

Although the broken remains of a small harbour can be seen at Port Mulgrave, access from the tiny village seems restricted. In fact the harbour was reached through underground tunnels originating far inland at the Grinkle ironstone mines, hence there was no need for any road link from the village. Ironstone was later removed from Grinkle by rail, and as the tunnel was no longer needed, it was closed, leaving the harbour unused by 1916.

The Cleveland Way is signposted off a corner of the road along the top of the rugged slope known as **Rosedale Cliffs**. Follow the path around **Lingrow Cliffs** to reach a small pond then turn right inland to return to the Runswick Bay Hotel. There are bus stops nearby on Ellerby Lane, or walkers could extend this route by immediately embarking on Walk 43.

WALK 43
Runswick Bay, Kettleness and Goldsborough

Distance	12.5km (7.75 miles)
Start/finish	Runswick Bay Hotel, GR 806161
Maps	OS Landranger 94; OS Explorer OL27 North.
Terrain	Easy walking, but the first part of the route is along a beach and is impassable at high tide; a cliff path gives way to paths inland, then an old railway trackbed starts firm and clear but later becomes overgrown
Refreshments	Pubs, restaurants and café at Runswick Bay, Fox and Hounds at Goldsborough
Transport	Regular Arriva buses link Runswick Bay with Whitby, Guisborough and Middlesbrough

The sandy beach walk around Runswick Bay is the only sandy beach in the whole guidebook, so make the most of it! A fine cliff walk continues around Kettleness, then the route heads inland to the little farming village of Goldsborough. After dropping back down to the village of Kettleness, the course of an old railway trackbed at first runs close to the coast, then swings inland in an enormous loop, crossing wooded valleys where views are more limited. This walk can be conveniently extended by linking with Walk 42.

Start at the **Runswick Bay Hotel** and follow the road past the Cliffemount Hotel, then walk down a narrow road closed to vehicles before continuing down to the beach at **Runswick Bay**. Note that onward progress might be blocked by a very high tide, in which case you could either wait for it to recede, maybe retreating to a pub or café, or reverse the entire route. Turn right to walk along the sandy beach, passing the blue-and-white **Runswick Bay Sailing Club** building at the far end. Continue past a

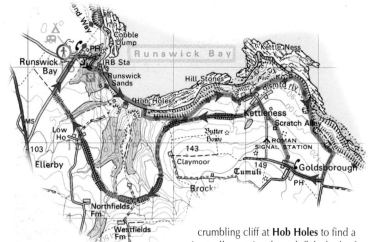

crumbling cliff at **Hob Holes** to find a
river valley cutting through flaky beds of
shale. Head inland through this valley,
holding onto ropes and scrambling up crum-
bling slopes of shale for a short while. A steep flight of
wooden steps leads up a bushy slope, out of the valley
and along the top of **High Cliff** around 100m (330ft).

Note the line of the **disused railway** a little further
inland. The cliff path is pushed inland a little by a small
gully choked with bushes. Turn left to follow a track
through the hamlet of **Kettleness**. Apart from the first
white building, keep seawards of all other buildings to
pick up the cliff path as marked later.

KETTLENESS

The bare, rugged headland of Kettle Ness was once worked for alum, jet and
ironstone. The previous village of Kettleness slumped into the sea in 1829,
but because the slump was gradual there was no loss of life, and the inhab-
itants were safely loaded onto a ship that was waiting for a consignment of
alum. The alum works were destroyed along with the village, but the slump
exposed more shale to be quarried, so a new works was built and operations
began again within two years.

After following the grassy cliff-top path around the **Kettle Ness** headland, note that the **disused railway** is close to hand again. Watch it carefully to see it disappear into a tunnel. The tunnel, or tunnels, since there are actually two of them, were cut after the original coastal railway was lost in a cliff-fall. Keep following the cliff path onwards, but watch out for a vague track running uphill and inland and follow it to a road corner. Turn right along the road to reach the little village of **Goldsborough**, where the Fox and Hounds is a sort of farmyard pub offering food, drink and accommodation.

The route climbs from the beach at Hob Holes onto the cliffs near Kettleness

Continue straight along the road signposted for Kettleness, but turn right, as indicated by a public footpath signpost, through a farmyard and down a grassy track. Veer slightly left across a large field of rough grazing, noting a mass of thistles on a hump where a **Roman signal station** was sited in 368 AD. A series of signal stations along the coast was linked via a line of sight through Hartlepool, Hunt Cliff, Boulby, Goldsborough, Whitby, Ravenscar, Scarborough and Filey. Cross a stile and walk down towards a chapel, then turn right down the road towards **Kettleness**. The first big building on the left is the old railway station, and before reaching it you should turn left to follow a clear track.

Continue along the old railway trackbed, which offers good views of the coast, at least while it runs near the cliffs – when the trackbed swings left inland, views become more restricted. Measure progress by ticking off **four stone arches** over the old line as the trackbed moves through bushy cuttings and has a grassy surface. The last arch is followed by a broad and muddy track that passes a house standing beside the old line. Continue straight along another grassy stretch where the path narrows considerably among nettles and brambles. However, the old line quickly leads to a road, dropping onto it where a bridge has been demolished. This is **Ellerby Lane** and a right turn along it leads straight back to the **Runswick Bay Hotel**.

RUNSWICK BAY

This delightful little village is stacked up a steep slope facing a curved bay with a fine sandy beach. Despite its obvious beauty, the situation looks precarious. One night in 1664, when most of the villagers were attending a funeral wake, the houses started to slip into the sea. By morning every dwelling was in ruins, except, for some mysterious reason, the dead man's house. Some claim that this house is the one now known as Jubilee Cottage. A sea wall protects the current village from landslip. A thatched cottage was formerly inhabited by the coastguard, who would have had one of the best vantage points to observe all the comings and goings around the bay.

WALK 44
Whitby, Saltwick Bay, Robin Hood's Bay and Hawsker

Distance	21km (13 miles)
Start/finish	Whitby Station, GR 898108
Maps	OS Landranger 94; OS Explorer OL27 North
Terrain	A moderate walk – urban walking gives way to a cliff coast path with a series of short ascents and descents; the second half of the walk uses a firm, clear and easy railway trackbed through cultivated countryside
Refreshments	Plenty of pubs, restaurants and cafés at Whitby and Robin Hood's Bay, pub and café at Saltwick Bay, pubs at Hawsker and Stainsacre
Transport	Regular Arriva buses link Whitby and Robin Hood's Bay with Scarborough, Guisborough and Middlesbrough

The cliff coast path from Whitby to Robin Hood's Bay is undoubtedly a classic short day's walk that could be accomplished in a morning or an afternoon, leaving plenty of time to explore the sights at either end. There are regular buses between both places too. However, there is also an old railway trackbed that once linked Robin Hood's Bay and Whitby, and this is now a Rail Trail available to walkers and cyclists. The trackbed is firm and clear throughout, rising and falling so gently that it might as well be level. Walkers using it pass an interesting station site at Stainsacre, and finish by crossing a towering brick viaduct high above the River Esk.

Start from the bus station or railway station in **Whitby** and walk along the harbour to reach the **Swing Bridge**, the lowest bridge in town. After crossing the bridge turn left along a narrow cobbled street lined with a variety of shops. Climb up the famous **199 steps** to reach St Mary's Church. Caedmon's Cross stands at the top of the steps,

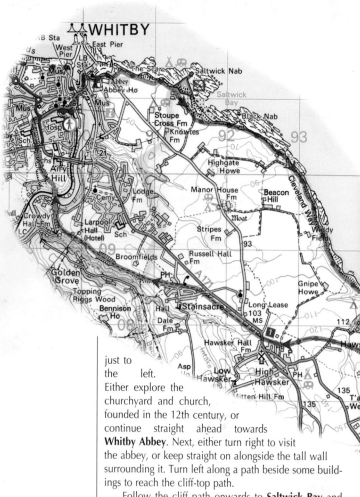

just to the left. Either explore the churchyard and church, founded in the 12th century, or continue straight ahead towards **Whitby Abbey**. Next, either turn right to visit the abbey, or keep straight on alongside the tall wall surrounding it. Turn left along a path beside some buildings to reach the cliff-top path.

Follow the cliff path onwards to **Saltwick Bay** and enjoy the open coastal scenery again. **Saltwick Nab** is a prominent humpbacked headland, but one that has largely resulted from the quarrying of alum shales. There

WHITBY ABBEY

St Hilda founded Whitby Abbey in 657 AD. According to legend, fossilised ammonites were said to be snakes that she turned to stone! The Danes destroyed the abbey in 867 AD and another foundation of 1078 was also unsuccessful. Much of what is seen today dates from the 12th century. However, the original abbey was founded in time to host the Synod of Whitby in 664 AD. This was when the Celtic and Roman Christian traditions, separated during the Dark Ages in Europe, settled some of the differences that each had accrued over the years, and agreed a method for calculating the movable feast of Easter. The abbey is also famous for one of its early lay brothers, Caedmon, who was inspired to sing in a dream one night, and whose words are the earliest written English Christian verse. There is an entrance charge, ☎ 01947 603568.

is access to the beach if required, otherwise walk along the road through the **Whitby Holiday Village**, where there is a campsite, shop, pub and café. Just as the road leaves the site a Cleveland Way signpost points left along the grassy cliff path. There is a view down on the isolated sea stack of **Black Nab**, also the result of alum shale quarrying. The twisted wreckage of the *Admiral Von Tromp*, which ran aground in 1976, can be seen near the beach.

Keep to the seaward side of a **foghorn**, but follow a path on the landward side of a **lighthouse**. Climb higher along the cliff path, to around 90m (295ft) above sea level. The path basically rolls along,

The atmospheric cliff-top ruins of Whitby Abbey stand high above Whitby town

rising and falling fairly gently, with rugged cliffs down to the left and fields rising to the right. There are, however, a couple of steep-sided wooded valleys to cross around **Maw Wyke Hole**. Also, at a point where a path heads inland to Hawsker, there is a bench and a small garden, but no habitation in view. The coast path climbs a bit, then swings round and down through a gentle valley at **Bay Ness**. Enjoy views back along the cliff coast. Walk around **Ness Point** to see Robin Hood's Bay, but only after passing below the old coastguard hut and entering the **Rocket Post Field**. The path runs to the top end of the village, at Mount Pleasant North, where you need to make a decision.

Either continue along a road and turn left to walk down through the higgledy-piggledy houses at **Robin Hood's Bay**, or simply turn right uphill and right again, barely setting foot on tarmac, to follow an old railway trackbed straight back to Whitby. (See Walk 45 for information about Robin Hood's Bay.)

A gravel track above Mount Pleasant North is sign-posted 'Railway Path'. Simply set off walking along the cinder trackbed to leave **Robin Hood's Bay**. The trackbed runs very gently uphill and there are no arches spanning the old line, nor does it cross any large bridges or have any deep cuttings. Views of the coast are gradually lost as the trackbed shifts inland by degrees. Pass some mobile homes near **Hawsker Bottoms**, around 125m (410ft), and cross a narrow road. There is a clear view ahead to Whitby Abbey and the gradient is now perceptibly gently downhill.

Go under a brick arch while passing the village of **Hawsker**. Cross the busy A171 using a pedestrian crossing, and maybe consider a detour into the village where the Hare and Hounds offers food and drink. Continuing along the old trackbed, the path is narrower until it passes the old railway station site at **Stainsacre**, which now operates as Trailways Cycle Hire. Later, cross a small iron bridge over a road and notice the **Windmill Inn** to the right.

Walk alongside a woodland, then go gently downhill through a wooded cutting before seeing open views towards Ruswarp and Eskdale on the left. Cross a monumental brick viaduct over the tidal **River Esk** and pass beneath three arches in a cutting that obscures views of **Whitby**. Pass beneath one final arch, then turn right down a flight of steps to reach a road. Walk down the road and go through a mini-roundabout as directed for the town centre. Note that the road passes **Pannett Park**, where there is an interesting museum, otherwise keep walking to return to the bus and railway stations.

Robin Hood's Bay with the rugged cliffs of Ravenscar seen in the distance

CAPTAIN COOK

After moving to Whitby from Staithes in 1747, James Cook was an apprentice seaman, lodging in an attic belonging to his Quaker master John Walker. The apprentices learned the art of navigation and seamanship through lessons, and hands-on experience on coal-carriers sailing to and from London. Cook's naval career began in 1755 and lasted for almost 25 years until his untimely death in Hawaii in 1779. It is no doubt a testimony to Whitby's shipbuilding expertise that four of Captain Cook's ships were built in the town: *Endeavour*, *Resolution*, *Discovery* and *Adventure*. A replica of *Endeavour* can be found in the harbour, where it can be boarded and inspected, and it often sails out of the harbour for short trips. The Captain Cook Memorial Museum on Grape Lane charts the life and times of this remarkable explorer. There is an entrance charge, ☎ 01947 601900.

WHITBY

As a town Whitby developed greatly from the mid-18th to mid-19th centuries, as its fishing fleets turned to whaling. Whalers spent months at sea and did not always return with a catch. Whale blubber was highly prized, as the oil rendered from it burned to give a bright and fairly soot-free light. Women of the era would have had more than enough reason to curse their whalebone corsets, but the trade allowed the town to prosper immensely. A fine whalebone arch was presented to the town in 1963 by Norway, suggesting that the Whitby whalers had long since disposed of every last part of their catch, bones and all! Facilities in Whitby include all types of accommodation, including a youth hostel and nearby campsite. There are banks with ATMs, a post office, toilets, and an abundance of pubs, restaurants, cafés, and takeaways. The tourist information centre is near Endeavour Wharf, ☎ 01947 602674.

WALK 45
Robin Hood's Bay, Boggle Hole and Ravenscar

Distance	14km (8.5 miles)
Start/finish	Station House, Robin Hood's Bay, GR 949054
Maps	OS Landranger 94; OS Explorer OL27 North
Terrain	Easy cliff coast walking with a few short steep ascents and descents, followed by field paths and a good, firm, clear railway trackbed
Refreshments	Pubs, restaurants and cafés at Robin Hood's Bay, Raven Hall Hotel and café at Ravenscar, Fylingdales Inn off-route at Fylingthorpe
Transport	Regular Arriva buses link Robin Hood's Bay with Whitby and Scarborough, Scarborough & District buses run between Ravenscar and Scarborough

The low cliff coast around Robin Hood's Bay is cleft by steep-sided wooded valleys at Boggle Hole and Stoupe Beck, but these are not particularly difficult to cross and the walk to the village of Ravenscar is easy enough. A splendid length of disused railway trackbed can be used further inland to return from Ravenscar to Robin Hood's Bay. The old line features quite noticeable gradients, though in effect the route might as well be level as far as walkers and cyclists are concerned. The line loops far inland to cross wooded valleys and pass through cuttings, finishing at an old station site.

Leave the car park near **Station House** at the top end of the village of **Robin Hood's Bay** and turn right at the Grosvenor Hotel. Walk down the B1447 and continue straight down a steep and narrow road, winding through the jumbled houses and cottages of the village to reach the rocky shore at a stout sea wall beside the **Bay Hotel**. Only a short way inland from the Bay Hotel the

215

Cleveland Way follows a narrow alley called **Albion Road**, then turns left up the stone **Flagstaff Steps**. Wooden steps climb higher on a bushy slope as the village is left behind. A level and easy low cliff walk is followed by a descent into a wooded valley. Cross a footbridge at **Boggle Hole Youth Hostel**, originally a corn mill, and follow the path uphill a short way to cross a beach access road and climb further.

Walk along the low cliff path, then down into another wooded valley to cross another footbridge over **Stoupe Beck**. Follow a narrow track, with flagstone steps alongside, up a wooded slope. Pass **Stoupe Bank Farm** and follow its access road until a slight dip has been crossed. Turn left as signposted Cleveland Way to pick up the cliff path again. Views back along the coast reveal that the village of Robin Hood's Bay is dwindling, while ahead the cliff-top village of Ravenscar draws nearer. The path is broad and grassy, running around 60m (200ft) above sea level. It suddenly heads uphill inland, through fields, then left along a **farm track**. Fork right up a **concrete track** at a junction, then fork right again up a **clear path** flanked by broom and gorse bushes. The path rises through woods and

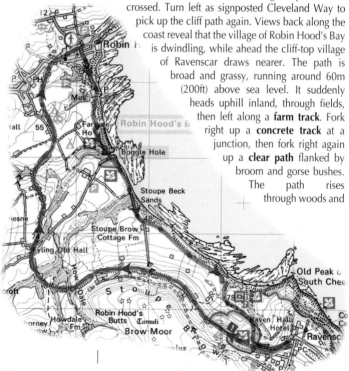

continues along a track studded with bricks that were made locally and stamped with the name **Ravenscar**. Walk up to the **National Trust Coastal Centre** near the entrance gate of the Raven Hall Hotel, around 190m (625ft). There are toilets nearby and a café along Station Road if needed.

RAVENSCAR

The Romans built a signal station at Ravenscar more or less where the Raven Hall Hotel now stands. Between 1600 and 1870 alum mining was a profitable occupation in the area, leaving the cliffs around Old Peak looking rather bare. In the 1890s there was a grand scheme to create a new tourist resort, but despite a road system and drains being laid, very few investors bought plots or built properties and the scheme ground to a halt in the 1920s. Ravenscar's history and heritage can be studied at the National Trust Coastal Centre.

Double back down the track from the **National Trust Coastal Centre** and step to the left onto the trackbed of an old railway line, signposted as the Rail Trail. It passes under an arch and runs very gently downhill in a cutting, passing the old **Brickyards Alum Quarry**. Gorse and broom grow alongside the old line, which soon begins to drift further inland. **Ewefield House** stands close to the trackbed, on the right, while **Browside Farm**, on the left, is an attractive huddle of buildings. The old line reaches its furthest point inland in a well-wooded area where it crosses **How Dale** and strides high above **Stoupe Beck**. Pass a bridge with three arches and there is a glimpse of **Fyling Old Hall** to the left. Steps lead down onto a road where a bridge has been demolished, and up the other side.

Fork right to continue along the old trackbed, passing the **Station Master's House**. Cross a minor road and pass **Middlewood Farm Holiday Park**, beyond which the trackbed becomes a tarmac path. Cross over a road between **Fylingthorpe** and Robin Hood's Bay and turn right to walk down the pavement

Robin Hood's Bay's cascade of houses is held in place by a stout sea wall

beside the road for a short way. Fork left to walk parallel to the road as marked, passing the old station site and Station House back at the car park and toilets at **Robin Hood's Bay**.

ROBIN HOOD'S BAY

This charming and curiously complex village has a history of smuggling, where the villagers often engaged in hostilities with the revenue men. Local folk claim that a bolt of silk could be passed through secret cupboards and doorways, from the shore to the top of the village, without once seeing the light of day! Local folk also tell of an incident when smugglers and revenue men waged a pitched battle in the bay and it was possible to read newsprint at night from the flash of gunpowder! The Bay Hotel rises straight from the rocky fossil-rich shore, and has had one ship wrecked against its wall as well as another poke its bowsprit straight through a window. One thing seems fairly certain – Robin Hood never had any association with the village.

WALK 46
Cloughton, Staintondale, Ravenscar and Hayburn Wyke

Distance	18km (11 miles)
Start/finish	Cloughton, GR 009947
Maps	OS Landrangers 94 and 101; OS Explorers OL27 South and OL27 North
Terrain	An easy, firm and level railway trackbed is used for the first half of the walk; a cliff coast path is used later, and this features a steep descent and ascent around Hayburn Wyke
Refreshments	Red Lion and Blacksmith's Arms at Cloughton, Falcon Inn off-route at Staintondale, Raven Hall Hotel and café at Ravenscar, and Hayburn Wyke Hotel at Hayburn Wyke
Transport	Regular Arriva buses link Cloughton with Scarborough and Whitby, and Scarborough & District buses link Ravenscar with Cloughton and Scarborough

Throughout this walk an old railway trackbed runs parallel to the cliff coast all the way between Cloughton and Ravenscar, and the distance between the old line and the cliff path is usually much less than 1km (0.5 mile). There are plenty of options to reduce the length of this walk simply by looking out for paths and tracks that cut across country from one half of the walk to the other. Anyone looking for a very short and scenic walk could turn off the line at the Hayburn Wyke Hotel and return quickly along the coast. The old line is known as the Rail Trail, while the cliff path is part of the Cleveland Way.

Leave the village of **Cloughton** by walking down Newlands Lane, passing nicely renovated buildings at **Court Green Farm**. When a bridge over an old railway trackbed is reached, turn left to walk down onto the old line and follow it onwards. The surface is level and cindery, and trees and bushes flank the line. Eventually pass **Northend House**,

219

which is on the right, then the route runs through a well-wooded stretch. Go through a gate and cross a road, where the **Hayburn Wyke Hotel** is just down to the right, offering food, drink and accommodation. There is easy access down to the beach at Hayburn Wyke, if any walkers wish to shorten the route considerably.

Continuing along the old line, note the old platform then go through another gate to head further through woodlands. Pass under a stone arch and later cross a wooded valley on a curved embankment. Go under another

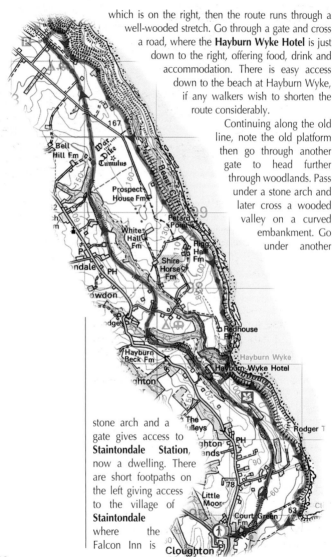

stone arch and a gate gives access to **Staintondale Station**, now a dwelling. There are short footpaths on the left giving access to the village of **Staintondale** where the Falcon Inn is

available. The trackbed later crosses another wooded valley, then goes through two gates where a farm track crosses the line. There are more open views of the immediate countryside. Go under another arch and eventually reach the old railway platform at **Ravenscar**, close to the Ravenscar Tea Rooms and a bus stop. The Raven Hall Hotel is located along Station Road if a visit is required.

Simply head straight from the tea rooms towards the cliffs and turn right to start following the coastal Cleveland Way. Follow the grassy cliff path roughly on a level, around 180m (590ft), then drop downhill a short way to enjoy views across a deep and wonderfully rugged hollow in the cliff face at **Blea Wyke Point**. The path runs above the wild and wooded slopes of **Beast Cliff**, designated a site of special scientific interest. **Prospect House Farm** stands fairly close to the cliffs, but other habitations are set well back. The path becomes something of a roller coaster and views ahead take in Scarborough Castle, Filey Brigg and Flamborough Head. After passing fairly close to **Redhouse Farm** the route descends steeply into a wooded valley using complex flights of wooden stairways and uneven stone steps. Cross a footbridge and consider a diversion down to the bouldery beach at **Hayburn Wyke**, where a small waterfall spills into a pool. (Hayburn Wyke Hotel and the Rail Trail are located only a short way inland.)

The rugged and wooded slopes of Beast Cliff are protected as a nature reserve

Climb uphill from the footbridge using stone steps, then turn left. Walk up more stone steps on a slope covered with intriguingly twisted corkscrew oaks and rhododendron. Watch for a junction of paths and keep right, moving further inland through the woods along the clearest path. Climb left up stone steps later, and turn left at the top. Climb further uphill to leave the woods and continue along the top of the wooded slope, looking back to the bay. When a grassy crest is reached at **Rodger Trod** there is a valley down to the right and the cliff coast to the left. Views ahead suggest a gentle descent, but the route is like a little roller coaster.

A low and easy cliff line leads round the rugged little bay at Cloughton Wyke

Turn right just before reaching the head of **Cloughton Wyke**, following a route indicated by yellow arrows. A footpath leads inland and gently uphill alongside a field. Turn right alongside the field, then step left through a gap to continue straight to a minor road. Turn left and follow the road, which crosses a bridge over the old railway trackbed. Simply continue past **Court Green Farm** and follow Newlands Lane back into the village of **Cloughton**.

THE RAIL TRAIL

The coastal railway between Scarborough and Whitby was engineered by John Waddell and ran from 1885. It brought places such as Robin Hood's Bay to the attention of tourists, but didn't seem to help plans for a resort at Ravenscar to get off the ground. The line was closed in 1965, but the trackbed remains open to walkers and cyclists as the Rail Trail, passing a handful of station sites and offering gentle gradients along the way. The full length of the line, along which it would be difficult to go astray, is about 30km (18.5 miles) and most reasonably fit walkers could cover the distance in a day. Occasionally hundreds of local schoolchildren use sections of the old railway line for sponsored walks.

THE LYKE WAKE WALK

Credit where credit is due: the Lyke Wake Walk is one of the great classic walks, not only of the North York Moors, but of Britain. It was first mooted by local farmer Bill Cowley in 1955 and completed for the first time soon afterwards. Half a century of trail history cannot be condensed here, but countless thousands of walkers have risen (and fallen) to the challenge of walking some 65km (40 miles) across the moors within a strict 24 hour time limit. Tales of hardship, heroism, record breaking, success and failure have become the stuff of legends over the decades, and there is no doubt whatsoever that the route has been an inspiration and challenge to walkers.

Since the death of Bill Cowley the numbers of walkers completing the Lyke Wake Walk have dwindled, but the route itself survives and the notion of completing it in 24 hours remains a stern challenge. However, maybe it is time for the route to be reappraised. After decades of self-inflicted hardship, perhaps walkers should take time to appreciate their surroundings and enjoy the whole walk in daylight, rather than struggling through the hours of darkness on some godforsaken moorland grind. While most reasonably fit walkers could cover the distance over a tough weekend, the idea of taking four days over the route really does allow for a pleasant and leisurely walk.

Taking four days means that additional distance will need to be covered in search of accommodation, since this is essentially a wild moorland route far from offers of food, drink and accommodation. In a couple of instances walkers might find it useful to time their arrival at certain roads in order to catch a bus to a nearby village for an overnight break. The first day's walk crosses the Cleveland Hills from Osmotherley to Clay Bank, where Moorsbus services offer descents to Chop Gate or Great Broughton. The second day's walk leads over the High Moors from Clay Bank to Blakey Ridge, where a pub and a house offer accommodation. The third day's walk crosses another empty stretch of the High Moors, from Blakey to Eller Beck, where walkers would should use Yorkshire Coastliner buses to reach villages off-route. The fourth and final day's walk from Eller Beck leads over the Eastern Moors to finish at Ravenscar, perched high above the Cleveland Coast.

Traditionalists may pour scorn on the notion of covering the Lyke Wake Walk in stages, but the aim is to *enjoy* the route and its wilderness surroundings, rather than *suffer* for the sake of meeting a deadline, walking through the night and seeing little of the remarkable moorland scenery. Most walkers who enjoy a fine

Lilla Cross stands on Lilla Howe and offers wide-ranging views across the moors (Walk 50)

day's walk will enjoy walking the Lyke Wake Walk in stages, and while they may find each daily stretch a tough undertaking, many of them would be happy not to increase their suffering fourfold!

The Lyke Wake Walk was named after the Cleveland Lyke Wake Dirge, a Yorkshire dialect verse describing the journey made across the dark and terrifying moors by a soul on its way to heaven or hell. There are several versions of the verse, which was already well established even in the 17th century, and may well be the oldest known dialect verse in Yorkshire.

WALK 47
Osmotherley, Carlton Bank, Cringle Moor and Hasty Bank

Distance	8km (11 miles)
Start	Market cross, Osmotherley, GR 456972
Finish	1257, Clay Bank, GR 573033
Maps	OS Landrangers 93 and 99; OS Explorer OL26 South and North
Terrain	A tough walk using a series of forest paths and hill paths, some of which are quite steep and rugged; the high moors are exposed.
Refreshments	Queen Catherine pub and cafés at Osmotherley, the Blacksmiths is off-route at Swainby, Lord Stones Café at Carlton Bank, and possibly a snack van at Clay Bank
Transport	Regular Abbott's bus services from Osmotherley to Northallerton and Stokesley, occasional Moorsbus services link Osmotherley with Carlton Bank and Chop Gate, and regular Moorsbus services cross Clay Bank to reach Great Broughton and Chop Gate

The first part of the Lyke Wake Walk is remarkably hilly, rather like a monstrous roller coaster running in tandem with the Cleveland Way over the Cleveland Hills. Strong walkers could combine this day's walk with the following day's walk to Blakey, but the total distance and the effort involved would be daunting for some. Breaking the journey at Clay Bank means that you have to follow the road one way or the other, to Great Broughton or Chop Gate, in search of accommodation. With reference to the Moorsbus timetable you can avoid the road walk by arriving at Clay Bank in time to catch a bus. Take careful note of the timetable as you need to return to Clay Bank again in the morning.

Leave **Osmotherley** by following the road called North End and turn left at the top of the village as signposted for the Cleveland Way. Follow a stony access road past a few houses, continuing uphill to a fork where the Cleveland Way is signposted to the left, running close to **Chapel Wood Farm**. Keep straight along the track, away from the farm, to reach a gate into **Arncliffe Wood**. Turn right up a clear path and continue along the inside edge of the wood, following a drystone wall over the crest of the hill. Pass the Telecom station on **Beacon Hill**, as well as a trig point at 299m (981ft). Drop downhill to reach a couple of gates leading onto heathery **Scarth Wood Moor**. Views ahead take in the hilly parts of the Lyke Wake Walk, with the little pyramidal peak of Roseberry Topping seen far ahead. A clear paved path runs down the moorland slope, then a left turn leads down a steeper pitched path to reach a minor road at **Scarth Nick**.

Cross a cattle-grid to find a signpost pointing along a clear woodland path at **Coalmire**. Continue straight along a woodland track, then later head down to the left. A stone at this point commemorates Bill Cowley, the local farmer who founded the Lyke Wake Walk. When a gate is reached at the bottom end of the wood there is access through it to the nearby village of **Swainby**, if refreshments are required, but turn right without going through the gate to stay inside the wood, enjoying the sight of huge oak trees. Watch for a left turn later which leads out of the wood and down through a field, linking with a track crossing two rivers in the wooded valley of **Scugdale**. Walk up a farm road to reach a road junction beside a telephone at **Huthwaite Green**.

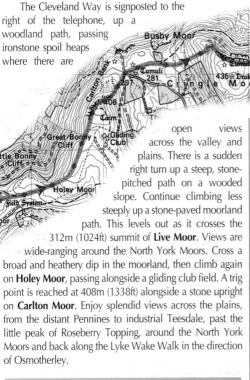

The Cleveland Way is signposted to the right of the telephone, up a woodland path, passing ironstone spoil heaps where there are

Map continues p.228

open views across the valley and plains. There is a sudden right turn up a steep, stone-pitched path on a wooded slope. Continue climbing less steeply up a stone-paved moorland path. This levels out as it crosses the 312m (1024ft) summit of **Live Moor**. Views are wide-ranging around the North York Moors. Cross a broad and heathery dip in the moorland, then climb again on **Holey Moor**, passing alongside a gliding club field. A trig point is reached at 408m (1338ft) alongside a stone upright on **Carlton Moor**. Enjoy splendid views across the plains, from the distant Pennines to industrial Teesdale, past the little peak of Roseberry Topping, around the North York Moors and back along the Lyke Wake Walk in the direction of Osmotherley.

A Lyke Wake Walk marker stone points the way towards the Cleveland Hills

Looking back along the route to Beacon Hill from the crest of Live Moor

Continued from p.227

Follow the stone-paved path steeply down to a gap, passing close to a quarried edge protected by a fence. Cross a track and a road on the lower slopes of **Carlton Bank**. Continue onwards, but note that there is immediate access to **Lord Stones Café** and toilets in a car park surrounded by trees. The café is not too apparent as it is largely buried underground!

Walk across a grassy common to leave the café, then follow a grassy track, flanked by a fence and drystone wall, through a gate, continuing up a paved path close to the wall. A stone **viewpoint seat** dedicated to local rambler Alec Falconer is reached at Cringle End. Climb higher along a gritty path and a paved path along the top of the abrupt northern edge of **Cringle Moor**, around 420m (1380ft). A steep, winding stone-pitched path leads downhill, passing shale spoil before reaching a fork on a gap. Keep right at the fork to go through a gate, then follow another steep, stone-pitched path over the top of **Cold Moor** at 401m (1316ft). Drop down to another gate and another grassy gap. The next steep climb passes to the left of the jagged, blocky **Wain Stones**, which are worth studying from all angles and completely out of character with the smooth contours of the North York Moors. Once above them a delightful level path runs along a moorland edge at 390m (1280ft) on **Hasty Bank**. At the end of this lofty promenade there is a steep path downhill, later following a wall down to the B1257 on **Clay Bank**.

Reaching the road on **Clay Bank** is not strictly the end of the day's walk. Strong walkers may well cross the road and continue onwards, while others will have studied the Moorsbus timetable and will catch a bus down to **Great Broughton** or **Chop Gate**, the two nearest villages, located in opposite directions, offering accommodation, food and drink. The only other alternative is to walk off-route to these places, which are both 4km (2.5 miles) off-route, a distance that might have to be repeated the following morning if there is no bus. A snack van might be available at a nearby forest car park on the Great Broughton side of the gap, but don't rely on this being present.

CHOP GATE

This hamlet is located down the road in Bilsdale, where facilities are limited to the Buck Inn, offering food, drink and accommodation. There are a couple of farmhouse around the dalehead.

GREAT BROUGHTON

This village is located down the road to the plains. The Wainstones Hotel offers food, drink and accommodation, the Bay Horse offers food and drink, and there are a couple of bed and breakfasts in the area as well as a post office shop.

WALK 48
Clay Bank, Urra Moor, Bloworth Crossing and Blakey

Distance	14km (8.75 miles)
Start	B1257, Clay Bank, GR 573033
Finish	Lion Inn, Blakey Ridge, GR 678997
Maps	OS Landrangers 93 and 94; OS Explorer OL26 North and South
Terrain	A moderate walk over high moors, mostly along good paths and tracks; the high moors are exposed
Refreshments	None along the route, then limited to the Lion Inn at the end of the day
Transport	Regular Moorsbus services cross Clay Bank from the nearby villages of Great Broughton and Chop Gate, and regular Moorsbus services run along Blakey Ridge, linking with Danby, Helmsley and Pickering

This is a lofty and remote part of the Lyke Wake Walk, traversing the highest part of the North York Moors and with no easy access to facilities of any kind. At the end of the day on Blakey Ridge, accommodation, food and drink are limited to only two establishments. Walkers who cannot secure lodgings and do not wish to cover any more of the route should check the Moorsbus timetables to reach nearby towns and villages. Paths and tracks are generally clear, but a wrong turning at a junction could involve a huge detour. In clear weather this is one of the most memorable parts of the route, especially when the heather moorlands are flushed purple in the summer.

Leave the B1257 on **Clay Bank** and follow a steep, stone-pitched path uphill alongside a wall. Go through a gate at the top of the slope and the path runs at an easier gradient across the higher moorlands. The broad crest is called **Carr Ridge** and rises around

Looking back along the stone-paved path from Carr Ridge across to Hasty Bank

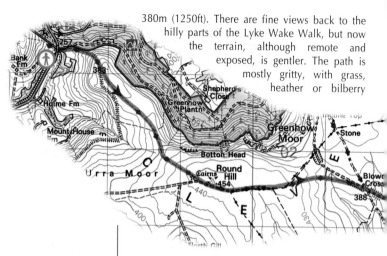

380m (1250ft). There are fine views back to the hilly parts of the Lyke Wake Walk, but now the terrain, although remote and exposed, is gentler. The path is mostly gritty, with grass, heather or bilberry alongside, although a few short stretches are paved with stone. Keep left, roughly along the crest of **Urra Moor**, until passing close to a trig point. This actually sits on a burial mound on **Round Hill** at 454m (1490ft) and can be reached by a short diversion along a path. It is the highest point on the moors, as well as in the whole of this guidebook! Note the **Hand Stone** and **Face Stone** beside the track, which are ancient route markers across the moor.

ROUND HILL

The trig point on Round Hill sits on the squat remains of a moorland burial mound. The North York Moors are dotted with similar mounds, and some parts are crisscrossed by ancient earthworks that were either territorial markers or defensive structures. The moorland marker known as the Hand Stone probably dates from the 18th century. It has two open palms with the near-indecipherable words: 'this is the way to Stoxla [Stokesley]' and 'this is the way to Kirbie [Kirkbymoorside]'. The older Face Stone features a crudely carved face.

Continue along the clearest track, then keep left at a fork. Later, cut across a moorland hollow, as marked, to reach an old railway trackbed. Turn right as signposted Cleveland Way and walk towards a barrier gate. Beyond the gate there is an intersection of tracks at **Bloworth Crossing**, at 388m (1773ft). The Cleveland Way turns left and is not seen again until Ravenscar, while the Lyke Wake Walk and

Map continues p.234

Coast to Coast Walk run straight ahead.

Pass another barrier gate to walk along the trackbed of the former Rosedale Railway. First walk along a low embankment, then pass through a shallow cutting as the track curves left. Cross a moorland beck on a little embankment, then the cutting at **Middle Head**, which can be a bit wet and muddy. The track curves and crosses another little embankment across another moorland beck, and enjoys fine views

Round Hill on Urra Moor is the highest point in the whole of the North York Moors

over Farndale from **Dale Head**. Gentle curves give way to a long low embankment which slips over the moorland crest so that you look down into Westerdale for a change. There is a junction with a clear track that leads down into the dale, but keep straight ahead.

The old railway trackbed rises very gently and overlooks Farndale again from **Farndale Moor**. On the way uphill there are more curves, then suddenly, as a shallow cutting is reached, the Lion Inn can be seen on a moorland crest across a valley. The trackbed makes a great curve around the valley and the inn passes from sight, but a **small outbuilding** remains visible and a path on the left climbs towards it. Keep to the left of the building, then turn right at the top of a drystone-walled enclosure. An old burial mound known as the **Cockpit** is reached just before the **Lion Inn**.

Continued from p.233

BLAKEY

Blakey is a bleak spot, but food, drink and accommodation are offered at the celebrated Lion Inn, at over 400m (1315ft). The inn was once popular with the coal and ironstone miners who worked on the moors, and is popular today with walkers and motorists. Accommodation is also available across the road at High Blakey House. Regular Moorsbus services link the inn with Danby, Helmsley and Pickering. Walkers following the Lyke Wake Walk have only three options: stay at the Lion Inn or High Blakey House across the road, or use the Moorsbus to reach some other place for accommodation.

WALK 49
Rosedale Head, Hamer, Wheeldale Moor and Simon Howe

Distance	22km (13.75 miles)
Start	Lion Inn, Blakey Ridge, GR 678997
Finish	Eller Beck Bridge, GR 858982
Maps	OS Landranger 94; OS Explorers OL26 North, OL27 North and OL27 South
Terrain	A tough walk over high moorlands but mostly on well-trodden paths, though some parts are rugged, boggy or vague, and care is needed with route-finding in places; the high moors are exposed
Refreshments	None along the route after leaving the Lion Inn
Transport	Regular Moorsbus services run along Blakey Ridge, linking with Danby, Helmsley and Pickering, and Yorkshire Coastliner buses run along the main road at Eller Beck Bridge, linking with Lockton, Pickering, Goathland and Whitby

This is a long and tough stage, where good weather helps enormously. The Lyke Wake Walk always stays on the high moors and pursues a direct course regardless of the nature of the terrain. Deeply worn paths can be muddy or stony underfoot, though sometimes the route can be a little vague too. Wheeldale Moor is particularly rough underfoot and should not be crossed in a hurry. Beyond Wheeldale the broad moor of Simon Howe is crossed with relative ease. However, Eller Beck Bridge is in the middle of nowhere and walkers must catch a bus elsewhere to find accommodation.

Leave the **Lion Inn** and walk along the road in the direction of Castleton. Watch for a bridleway signposted off to the right, where a trodden path crosses a dip in the moorlands at **Rosedale Head**, passing a couple of chunky boundary stones before rising back to a road. Have a look

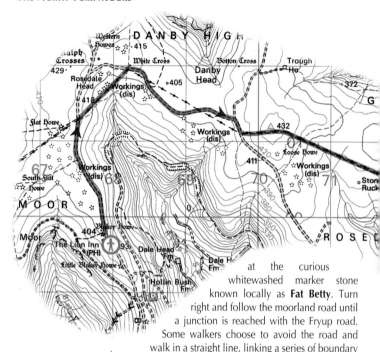

at the curious whitewashed marker stone known locally as **Fat Betty**. Turn right and follow the moorland road until a junction is reached with the Fryup road. Some walkers choose to avoid the road and walk in a straight line, linking a series of boundary stones with whitewashed tops. The Coast to Coast Walk turns left at the road junction and is not seen again.

Take note of a moorland marker, in the shape of a huge **standing stone**, planted at this junction by the North York Moors Authority in the year 2000. It serves to illustrate that the tradition of erecting stones on these bleak moors still lives! Follow the Rosedale road onwards a little, then turn left up the only clear path in sight. This path has been deeply eroded into a stony or peaty groove up the heather slopes of **Seavey Hill**. (Note how it follows the line of white-topped boundary stones.) Cross over a rise at 432m (1417ft) and walk downhill to pass the larger **Causeway Stone**, where a flagstone causeway slices across the moorland. The Lyke Wake Walk is at first broad and eroded, then crosses a wide sodden rushy dip on the moor.

Climb gently up another slope beyond, then gradients are barely perceptible across **Rosedale Moor**. The path remains broad and clear and is generally firm underfoot as it forges through the heather, around 390m (1280ft). Cross the gentle valley of **North Gill** where a shooting hut can be seen well away to the right. Head uphill and across a broad moorland to reach the prominent cairn on top of the heathery bump of **Shunner**

Howe, over 360m (1280ft). There are views back across the day's walk, as well as ahead to Lilla Howe.

Map continues p.238

Walk down the gently graded stony path towards a road. Avoid the green space near the scant ruins of an old inn at **Hamer**, and aim to keep left along a lesser path to reach the road near a small parking space.

Cross the road and walk through a rushy patch, then follow a clear but occasionally rugged moorland path through the heather on **Hamer Moor**. Some parts of the path have been surfaced with gravel or duckboards, but these are wearing out, leaving bare peat that can be wet in places. On the higher parts of **White Moor** the ground is bouldery, and the prominent standing stone of **Blue Man-i'-th'-Moss** is reached (traces of blue paint that once covered the stone can be distinguished). Nearby is the heathery hump of Wheeldale Howe at 318m (1043ft),

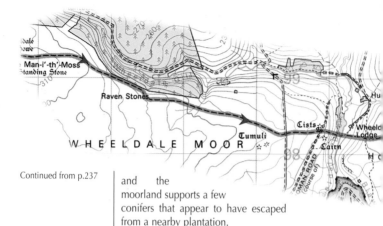

Continued from p.237

and   the moorland supports a few conifers that appear to have escaped from a nearby plantation.

Watch carefully to spot the line of a narrow path as it crosses very rough and bouldery moorland that has plenty of wet patches. The path narrows as it runs closer to **Wheeldale Plantation**, then drifts away from the forest and becomes broader. Keep following it and the terrain eases as **Wheeldale Moor** slopes gradually down to a minor road. Cross the road and go over a stile over a fence to continue downhill alongside a fence. Cross over ancient **Wheeldale Road** and continue downhill, soon picking a way down a steep and bouldery slope covered in bracken. Stone steps lead to **Wheeldale Beck** and step-

The Lyke Wake Walk crosses stepping stones over Wheeldale Beck

238

ping stones lead across to the other side. A prominent building nearby, **Wheeldale Lodge**, previously served as a youth hostel.

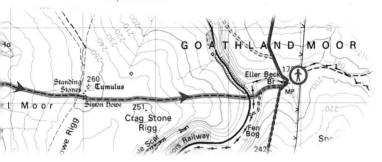

Cross a step-stile and follow a path up another slope of bracken. Step across a track and walk up past a rocky brow to reach a large cairn where heather moorland stretches ahead. Simply follow the path, which is fairly easy and obvious, though wet in places, up to a cairn on top of **Simon Howe**. There is a trig point off-route at 260m (853ft), but it doesn't have to be visited. Enjoy views around the higher moors, whose near-horizontal lines are broken only by the pyramid at RAF Fylingdales. Keep walking straight ahead to descend gradually on the moorland slope. The path steepens a little to cross a stile, and you should watch and listen for trains while crossing the North Yorkshire Moors Railway line. A path made of railway sleepers crosses the Fen Bog Nature Reserve and leads up to another stile. Walk along a track to reach the busy A169 at **Eller Beck Bridge**.

Due to the nature of the road, which bends across the bridge, buses are unlikely to stop at this point to deal with prospective passengers. Cross the bridge, therefore, and walk with care up the right-hand side of the busy road, turning left along the road signposted for Goathland. Buses can stop safely here and walkers can use them to reach Goathland, in the Whitby direction, or Lockton, in the Pickering direction, in search of accommodation.

WALK 50
Eller Beck, Lilla Howe, Jugger Howe Moor and Ravenscar

Distance	14km (8.75 miles)
Start	Eller Beck Bridge, GR 858982
Finish	Raven Hall Hotel, Ravenscar, GR 980017
Maps	OS Landranger 94; OS Explorer OL27 South and North
Terrain	A tough walk over high moorlands, but mostly along good paths and tracks; the high moors are exposed
Refreshments	None along the route, though the Flask Inn can be reached off-route on the A171, and the Raven Hall Hotel and a café are available at the finish in Ravenscar
Transport	Yorkshire Coastliner buses cross Eller Beck Bridge between Pickering and Whitby, regular Arriva buses run from the Flask Inn (on the A171) to Whitby and Scarborough, and Scarborough & District buses link Ravenscar with Scarborough

The last part of the Lyke Wake Walk traverses a broad moorland crowned by Lilla Cross. Views back along the route and ahead reveal how astonishingly direct the route really is. Walkers have to cross the rugged valley drained by Jugger Howe Beck to continue, then climb gently over one last moorland to gain a view of their ultimate destination – Ravenscar. Over the past decades most Lyke Wake Walk participants have been content to limp down the road to finish, but with more time at your disposal you can link together paths and tracks and complete the walk at a leisurely pace, and explore the village too.

Walkers reaching Eller Beck Bridge by bus should note that buses cannot stop safely, so alight at the nearby road junction for Goathland. Go down the busy **A169**, walking with care along the right-hand side, facing the traffic, to cross **Eller Beck Bridge**. Turn left to leave the

road and follow a track that is clearly marked as
running onto **MOD property** – part of RAF Fylingdales.
Cross a stile beside a gate and walk beneath a pylon
line to the end of the track. Keep to the left-hand side
of a fence to continue, following a path across a boggy
area full of bog myrtle. The path aligns itself to **Little
Eller Beck** and pulls away from the fence. There is a
line of white posts planted all the way up the heather
moorland slope, and the path is always well to the left
of them. It can be muddy underfoot in places, but later
a firm gravel track is reached and a left turn leads to a
gate. Go through the gate and cross another track,
walking straight ahead up a more rugged path on a
heathery slope. Cross a rugged track, then aim for **Lilla
Cross** on Lilla Howe, at 292m (958ft). Although of no
great height, this moorland top offers extensive views
through the heart of the North York Moors.

Walk straight ahead down the path from Lilla Howe,
keeping right along a track to reach a track junction
where there is a **boulder**. Branch left along a track that
can be rough and stony, as well as muddy when wet, but
it is clear and obvious as it descends gently over
Fylingdales Moor, passing a cairn on a mound known as
Burn Howe. The track becomes a narrow path, but
remains clear to follow, becoming quite rugged then
steepening as it drops towards

Map continues p.242

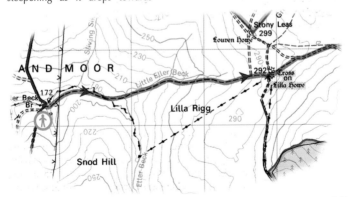

View back across the moors traversed by the Lyke Wake Walk near Ravenscar

Jugger Howe Beck. Cross the wet and muddy land near the beck and cross the beck too. Follow a path straight uphill among bracken and heather on **Jugger Howe Moor**. Walk along a clear track that becomes a concrete road leading to a gate. Cross a road that was formerly the main road, then cross the rather busy **A171** with care.

Continued from p.241

Note that a left turn along the main road leads to the Flask Inn, which offers accommodation, food and drink. There are buses along this road, though it may be difficult to stop them at any point other than the bus stops at the Flask Inn.

The route climbs straight up the banking above the main road, then follows a narrow path across **Stony Marl Moor**. A substantial part of the moorland has been burnt, and if the heather does not regenerate it will become a grassy area. Later the moorland is heathery, and as height is gained a clear track forms and leads close to a **trig point** before landing on a minor road beside a tall communication mast. The height at this point is 266m (873ft), and not only are there are no more hills to climb, the finishing point is clearly in view!

For the descent turn left along the road, then almost immediately branch right along a narrow path signposted as a

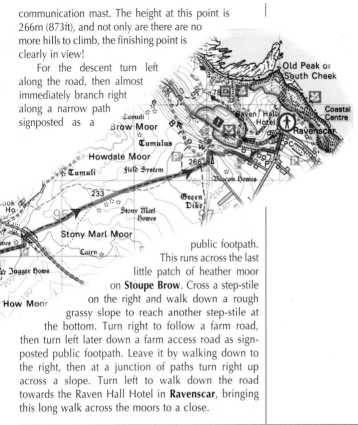

public footpath. This runs across the last little patch of heather moor on **Stoupe Brow**. Cross a step-stile on the right and walk down a rough grassy slope to reach another step-stile at the bottom. Turn right to follow a farm road, then turn left later down a farm access road as signposted public footpath. Leave it by walking down to the right, then at a junction of paths turn right up across a slope. Turn left to walk down the road towards the Raven Hall Hotel in **Ravenscar**, bringing this long walk across the moors to a close.

CAUTIONARY TALE

Those who insist on covering the whole of the Lyke Wake Walk in 24 hours are reminded of a short conversation that took place a long time ago between a customer and a former proprietor in the café at Ravenscar:

'You must see some funny sights coming in here.'

'Yes, but they're funnier still when they try to get up to go out.'

APPENDIX 1: BRIEF HISTORY OF THE MOORS

Early Settlement

The first people to roam across the North York Moors were Mesolithic nomads, eking out an existence as hunter-gatherers some 10,000 years ago. Swampy lowlands surrounded the uplands at that time, and apart from a few flakes of flint these people left little trace of their passing. Neolithic settlers piled mounds of stones over their burial sites and these long barrows date back to 2000 BC. Soon afterwards, from 1800 BC, there were greater numbers of settlers as the Beaker people and Bronze Age invaders moved into the area. They used more advanced methods of land clearance and tillage, and buried their dead in conspicuous mounds known as 'howes', often in high places. These people over-developed the land, clearing too much forest too quickly, and minerals leached from the thin soils so that the uplands became unproductive. Climate changes led to ground becoming waterlogged and mossy, so that tillage became impossible and scrub moorland developed. Iron Age people had more of a struggle to survive and had to organise themselves in defensive promontory forts. Perhaps some of the linear dykes that cut across the countryside date from that time, though many structures are difficult to date with any degree of certainty.

Roman Settlement

The Romans pushed through Britain in the 1st century and founded a splendid city at York. Perhaps the most important site on the North York Moors was Cawthorn Camp near Cropton, used as a military training ground by Roman soldiers. Although Wade's Causeway in Wheeldale is often referred to as a Roman road, recent thinking suggests it may not be. Hadrian's Wall kept the Picts at bay to the north, but the east coast was open to invasion by the Saxons. The Romans built several coastal signal stations, each linked to the other by a line of sight. These were founded in 368 AD at Hartlepool, Hunt Cliff, Boulby, Goldsborough, Whitby, Ravenscar, Scarborough, Filey and Flamborough Head. Some of these sites have been lost as the cliffs have receded, while excavations at a couple of sites suggest that those keeping a lookout met a sudden and bloody end. By 410 AD the Romans had left and the coast was literally clear for wave upon wave of invasion.

Dark Age Settlement

Saxons, Angles, Danes and other invaders left their mark on the North York Moors, establishing little villages and tilling the land, mostly in the dales, as the higher ground had long reverted to scrub. Many of these settlers were Christian, and in 657 AD an important monastery was founded in the Celtic Christian tradition at Whitby. Whitby Abbey was notable for one of its early lay brothers, Caedmon, who was inspired to sing, and whose words are the earliest written English Christian verse. There were times of strife during the successive waves of invasion and the abbey was destroyed in 867 AD. Other rural monastic sites are known, all on a small scale, and many of the early Christian churches were simple wooden buildings. Some of the earliest carved stone crosses date from the 10th century.

Norman Settlement

A more comprehensive invasion was mounted by the Normans, who swept through the region in the 11th century and completely subdued it. They totally reorganised society, establishing the feudal system and leaving an invaluable insight into the state of the countryside by listing vast numbers of settlements and properties in the *Domesday Book*. In return for allegiance to the king, noblemen were handed vast tracts of countryside and complete dominion over those who lived there. Resentment and violence was rife for a time and the new overlords were obliged to build themselves castles. Many noblemen in turn gifted large parts of their estates to various religious orders from mainland Europe, encouraging them to settle in the area.

Monastic Settlement

Great monasteries and abbeys were founded in and around the North York Moors in the wake of the Norman invasion, and ruins dating from the 12th and 13th centuries still dominate the countryside. Stone quarrying was important at this time, and large-scale sheep rearing was developed, so the dales began to feature large, close-cropped pastures. There were still plenty of woodlands for timber and hunting, but the moors remained bleak and barren, and were reckoned to be of little worth. Early maps and descriptions by travellers simply dismissed the area as 'black-a-moor', yet it was necessary for people to cross the moors if only to get from place to place, and a network of paths developed. The monasteries planted some of the old stone crosses on the moors to provide guidance to travellers. This era came to a sudden close with Henry VIII's dissolution of the monasteries in the 16th century.

The towering arches of Rievaulx Abbey

Recent Settlement

In the past few centuries the settlement of the North York Moors has been influenced by its mineral wealth and by the burgeoning tourist industry. At the beginning of the 17th century an amazing chemical industry developed to extract a highly prized salt known as 'alum' from a particular deposit of shale. This industry lasted two and a half centuries and had a huge impact on the landscape around the cliff-bound fringes of the North York Moors. From the mid-18th to mid-19th centuries, Whitby's fishing industry specialised in whaling, and the town benefited greatly from the trade. The 19th century was the peak period for jet production, often referred to as 'Whitby jet'. Railways were built in and around the North York Moors through the 19th century, bringing an increase in trade and allowing easier shipment of local ironstone from the moors. Railways also laid the foundations for a brisk tourist trade, bringing new life to coastal resorts whose trade and fishing fleets were on the wane. Tourism continues to be one of the most important industries in the area, and tourism in the countryside is very much dependent on walking.

APPENDIX 2: NORTH YORK MOORS INDUSTRIES

Alum

Throughout the North York Moors National Park huge piles of flaky pink shale have been dumped on the landscape, sometimes along the western fringes of the Cleveland Hills, but more especially along the coast. These are the remains of a large-scale chemical industry that thrived from 1600 to 1870. The hard-won prize was alum, a salt that could be extracted from certain beds of shale by a tortuous and time-consuming process.

Wherever the shale occurred it was extensively quarried. Millions of tons were cut, changing the shape of the landscape considerably, especially along the coast. Wood, and in later years coal, was mixed in layers with the broken shale, and huge piles like small hills were fired and kept burning for months, or even a whole year. Burnt shale was put into huge tanks of water to soak, a process known as 'leaching'. The water was drawn off and boiled, which required more wood and coal, as well as treatment with such odious substances as human urine, brought to the area from as far away as London. As crystals of the precious alum began to form, the process ended with a stage of purification before the end product was packed for dispatch.

Alum had many uses, but was chiefly in demand as a fixative for dyes, allowing cloth to be strongly coloured and colour-fast after washing. The Italians had a virtual monopoly on the trade until the alum shale of Yorkshire was exploited from 1600. The local industry went into a sudden decline when other sources of alum, and more advanced dyestuffs, were discovered from 1850. The long and involved process of quarrying, burning, leaching, boiling, crystallisation and purification was replaced by simpler, cheaper and faster means of production. There are some two dozen sites scattered across the landscape where the industry flourished. Look on these stark remains, consider the toil and labour, and bear in mind that it all took place so that the fine gentlemen and ladies could wear brightly coloured clothes!

Jet

Jet, often known as Whitby jet, has been used to create ornaments and jewellery since the Bronze Age. It is found in certain beds of rock that outcrop around the North York Moors, often along the coast, but also far inland around Carlton Bank.

Basically jet is nothing more than a type of coal, but it is peculiar because it has formed from isolated logs of driftwood rather than from the thick masses of decayed vegetation that form regular coal seams. High-quality jet is tough and black, can be turned on a lathe or carved, and takes a high polish. Jet has been used to create everything from intricately carved statuettes to shiny beads and facetted stones for jewellery. Jet crafting has long centred on Whitby, with peak production years being in the 19th century.

Ironstone
Cleveland ironstone was mined and quarried from around 500 BC, as evidenced by an ancient bloomery site (where malleable iron is produced directly from iron ore) on Levisham Moor. However, large-scale working didn't commence until around 1850, when moorland and coastal locations such as Skinningrove and Rosedale were exploited. The tiny coastal village of Skinningrove became the 'valley of iron' as a major steelworks was developed. Ironstone from Rosedale was transported over the moors by rail to be loaded into the blast furnaces at Middlesbrough. Huge quantities of coal had to be shipped to the area, while industry and commerce were hungry for the iron that was produced. The last local ironstone mine, at North Skelton, closed in 1964. Steelworks at Middlesbrough are now much reduced, while Skinningrove only just manages to remain in production.

Fishing and Whaling
The coastal towns and villages thrived on fishing, and especially herring fishing, until stocks dwindled. In Whitby, mainly from the mid-18th to mid-19th centuries, the fishing fleets turned their attention to whaling. Whalers spent months at sea and did not always return with a catch, but regular catches brought great wealth to the town. Whale blubber was rendered for its oil, which was highly prized, because when it burned it gave a bright and fairly soot-free light. Women of the era would have had more than enough reason to curse their whale-bone corsets, but the trade allowed the town to prosper immensely. Whenever the fishing settlements fell on hard times, smuggling provided an alternative form of employment, most notably at Robin Hood's Bay.

Grouse Shooting
What of the heather moorlands at the heart of the North York Moors National Park? While some visitors imagine that the moors have always been there, and represent the true wilderness qualities of the area, this is quite untrue. The moors have been man-managed over a long period of time and will only continue to exist as they do with year-round maintenance. If the stark truth be known, those

uniform heather moorlands are largely a 19th-century creation, managed entirely for the sport of grouse shooting!

The red grouse is essentially a British bird, tied to the heather moorlands on which it depends for food and shelter. Walkers know it well for its heart-stopping habit of suddenly breaking cover from beneath their feet, then flying low while calling 'go-back, go-back, go-back'. It is a wonderfully camouflaged bird, spending all its time among the heather. Grouse graze on young heather shoots, but need deep heather for shelter and to evade predators. Natural moorlands present a mosaic of vegetation types, but as the sport of grouse shooting developed in the 19th century it became clear that a uniform heather habitat favouring the grouse above all other species would result in much greater numbers of birds to shoot!

Moorland management required vegetation to be periodically burnt, and as heather seeds are more fire-resistant than other seeds, heather cover quickly became dominant. Drainage ditches were dug through bogs to dry the ground and encourage further heather growth. Heather was burnt and regrown on a slow rotation basis to provide short heather for feeding and deep 'leggy' heather for shelter. Gamekeepers were employed to shoot or trap 'vermin' so that grouse could flourish free of their predators, but it remains difficult to control the intestinal parasites that often result in the birds being in poor condition. Harsh winters and cold wet springs cause devastating losses among populations of grouse. Latterly the old paths used by shooting parties have been widened for vehicular use, sometimes rather insensitively.

Come 'the glorious twelfth', or 12 August, the grouse-shooting season opens with teams of beaters driving the grouse towards the shooters, who station themselves behind shooting butts. Some moorlands charge very high prices for a day's shooting, and shoots are very much a social occasion. Walkers who despise blood sports should nevertheless bear in mind that without grouse shooting the moors would not be managed and would revert to scrub. A lot of moorland has been lost to forestry and agriculture, and to a certain extent managing the moors for grouse shooting prevents any further loss. What remains today is England's greatest unbroken expanse of heather moorland, and most visitors are keen to see it preserved as such.

North York Moors Today

The North York Moors National Park Authority maintains an up-to-date website full of current contact information, events information, and a comprehensive wealth of notes that go well beyond the scope of this guidebook. Be sure to check it in advance of any visit at **www.moors.uk.net**.

APPENDIX 3: ROUTE SUMMARY

Walk		Distance	
The Tabular Hills			
Walk 1	West Ayton, Hackness and the Forge Valley	15km	9.5 miles
Walk 2	Hackness, Broxa and Whisper Dale	10km	6 miles
Walk 3	Lockton, Stain Dale, Saltergate and Levisham Moor	20km	12.5 miles
Walk 4	Levisham and the Hole of Horcum	13km	8 miles
Walk 5	Levisham Station, Levisham and Newton-on-Rawcliffe	10km	6 miles
Walk 6	Hutton-le-Hole, Lastingham, Cropton and Appleton-le-Moors	16km	10 miles
Walk 7	Gillamoor, Boonhill Common and Fadmoor	8km	5 miles
Walk 8	Newgate Bank, Rievaulx Moor and Helmsley Bank	18km	11 miles
Walk 9	Helmsley, Beck Dale and Ash Dale	11km	6.5 miles
Walk 10	Hawnby Hill and Easterside Hill	7.5km	4.5 miles
The Hambleton Hills			
Walk 11	Rievaulx Abbey and Old Byland	12km	7.5 miles
Walk 12	Byland Abbey, Mount Snever and Oldstead	8km	5 miles
Walk 13	Sutton Bank, Gormire Lake and the White Horse	15km	9.5 miles
Walk 14	Osmotherley, Thimbleby, Siltons and Black Hambleton	19km	12 miles
The Cleveland Hills			
Walk 15	Osmotherley, Beacon Hill and High Lane	13km	8 miles
Walk 16	Chop Gate, Cringle Moor and Cock Howe	16km	10 miles
Walk 17	Chop Gate, Urra Moor, Hasty Bank and Cold Moor	15km	9.5 miles
Walk 18	Kildale, Ingleby Moor and Battersby Moor	17km	10.5 miles
Walk 19	Kildale, Leven Vale, Baysdale and Hograh Moor	16km	10 miles
The Northern Moors			
Walk 20	Great Ayton, Easby Moor and Roseberry Topping	11km	6.5 miles
Walk 21	Guisborough, Gisborough Moor and Hutton Village	15km	9.5 miles
Walk 22	Danby, Siss Cross, Commondale and Castleton	14km	8.75 miles
Walk 23	Scaling Dam, Clitherbeck, Danby and Beacon Hill	14km	8.75 miles

Walk		Distance	
The High Moors			
Walk 24	Chop Gate, Cock Howe, Ryedale and Wetherhouse Moor	20km	12.5 miles
Walk 25	Chop Gate, Tripsdale, Bransdale and Bilsdale	18km	11 miles
Walk 26	Low Mill, Harland, Rudland Rigg and West Gill	16km	10 miles
Walk 27	Church Houses, Bloworth Crossing and Farndale Moor	20km	12.5 miles
Walk 28	Hutton-le-Hole, Ana Cross, Spaunton Moor and Lastingham	13km	8 miles
Walk 29	Rosedale, Hartoft, Lastingham and Ana Cross	14km	8.75 miles
Walk 30	Rosedale Ironstone Railway around Rosedale Head	19km	12 miles
Walk 31	Rosedale Ironstone Railway from Blakey to Battersby	17km	10.5 miles
Walk 32	Westerdale, Fat Betty, Westerdale Moor and Esklets	15km	9.5 miles
Walk 33	Danby, Castleton, Botton Village and Danby Rigg	16km	10 miles
Walk 34	Lealholm, Heads, Glaisdale Moor and Glaisdale Rigg	22.5km	14 miles
Walk 35	Glaisdale Rigg, Egton High Moor and Egton Bridge	21km	13 miles
The Eastern Moors			
Walk 36	Goathland, Simon Howe, Wheeldale and Mallyan Spout	15km	9.5 miles
Walk 37	Historic Railway Walk from Moorgates to Grosmont	8km	5 miles
Walk 38	Goathland, Goathland Moor and the Whinstone Ridge	6.5km	4 miles
Walk 39	Goathland, Eller Beck, Lilla Howe and Goathland Moor	17km	10.5 miles
Walk 40	Chapel Farm, Lilla Howe and Jugger Howe Beck	17km	10.5 miles
Walk 41	Sleights, Ugglebarnby, Falling Foss and Littlebeck	13km	8 miles
The Cleveland Coast			
Walk 42	Runswick Bay, Hinderwell, Staithes and Port Mulgrave	11.5km	7 miles
Walk 43	Runswick Bay, Kettleness and Goldsborough	12.5km	7.75 miles
Walk 44	Whitby, Saltwick Bay, Robin Hood's Bay and Hawsker	21km	13 miles
Walk 45	Robin Hood's Bay, Boggle Hole and Ravenscar	14km	8.5 miles
Walk 46	Cloughton, Staintondale, Ravenscar and Hayburn Wyke	18km	11 miles
The Lyke Wake Walk			
Walk 47	Osmotherley, Carlton Bank, Cringle Moor and Hasty Bank	18km	11 miles
Walk 48	Clay Bank, Urra Moor, Bloworth Crossing and Blakey	14km	8.75 miles
Walk 49	Rosedale Head, Hamer, Wheeldale Moor and Simon Howe	22km	13.75 miles
Walk 50	Eller Beck, Lilla Howe, Jugger Howe Moor and Ravenscar	14km	8.75 miles

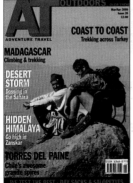

LISTING OF CICERONE GUIDES

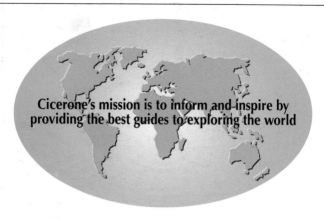

Cicerone's mission is to inform and inspire by providing the best guides to exploring the world

Since its foundation over 30 years ago, Cicerone has specialised in publishing guidebooks and has built a reputation for quality and reliability. It now publishes nearly 300 guides to the major destinations for outdoor enthusiasts, including Europe, UK and the rest of the world.

Written by leading and committed specialists, Cicerone guides are recognised as the most authoritative. They are full of information, maps and illustrations so that the user can plan and complete a successful and safe trip or expedition – be it a long face climb, a walk over Lakeland fells, an alpine traverse, a Himalayan trek or a ramble in the countryside.

With a thorough introduction to assist planning, clear diagrams, maps and colour photographs to illustrate the terrain and route, and accurate and detailed text, Cicerone guides are designed for ease of use and access to the information.

If the facts on the ground change, or there is any aspect of a guide that you think we can improve, we are always delighted to hear from you.

Cicerone Press
2 Police Square Milnthorpe Cumbria LA7 7PY
Tel:01539 562 069   Fax:01539 563 417
e-mail:info@cicerone.co.uk   web:www.cicerone.co.uk